Praise for *Soar* ...

'... *Soar* is refreshingly candid and immediate. It's often a great deal of fun too.'

—Deborah Jones, *The Australian*

'McAllister's tone is light, friendly and always fair. This is not a book of scuttlebutt and gossip. McAllister's exuberant dancing and his love of the artform were infectious; he has given much joy to the world. Now he steps into another phase of his career, with the man he loves by his side.'

—Karen van Ulzen, *Dance Australia*

'It is excellently written in a warm, friendly tone. Some of it is incredibly, intimately frank and revealing. *Soar* opens dramatically with [David McAllister's] first sexual experience, fixing the idea in the reader's mind that the book is not just about his career but McAllister's long-term fight struggling to acknowledge his sexuality – to himself and others. *Soar* is also a fascinating insight into the stresses and successes of being an Artistic Director.'

—Lynne Lancaster, *Sydney Arts Guide*

'It's this incautious and refreshing openness, especially about his sexuality, that makes McAllister's memoir rewarding reading. *Soar* is a book for those with a curiosity about ballet's backstage, served with a side of self-reckoning.'

—Nathan Smith, *Books + Publishing*

'Bright and brisk, David McAllister's autobiography *Soar: A Life Freed by Dance* nimbly chronicles the sacrifices, setbacks and successes of a life devoted to dance. Supportively co-authored by journalist Amanda Dunn, *Soar* is told in the warm tone of McAllister's voice, giving the reader the sense of being humbly regaled on decades of dance as well as being taken into highly personal confidences of life beyond the footlights.'

—Simon Parris, *Man in Chair*

'There's almost a fairytale quality to McAllister's triumphant story – princesses and romance included. What a supple testament to the pursuit of beauty, the importance of art, and the discipline required to answer your calling.'

—Benjamin Law

'I loved *Soar* ... so entertaining and fascinating ... what an amazing career and so well-deserved, and the personal story so beautiful and shy ... David is so bloody talented in so many areas ... can even write a ripping memoir.'

—Jane Turner

DAVID McALLISTER

SOAR

A LIFE FREED BY DANCE

with Amanda Dunn

To Mum and Dad, whose love and belief gave
me the confidence to fly

First published in Australia in 2020
by Thames & Hudson Australia Pty Ltd
11 Central Boulevard, Portside Business Park
Port Melbourne, Victoria 3207
ABN: 72 004 751 964

This edition first published in 2021

thamesandhudson.com.au

24 23 22 21 5 4 3 2 1

Thames & Hudson Australia wishes to acknowledge that Aboriginal and Torres Strait Islander people are the first storytellers of this nation and the traditional custodians of the land on which we live and work. We acknowledge their continuing culture and pay respect to Elders past, present and future.

ISBN 978-1-760-76227-8 (paperback)

ISBN 978-1-760-76104-2 (hardback)

ISBN 978-1-760-76135-6 (ebook)

A catalogue record for this book is available from the National Library of Australia

Cover image: *David McAllister*, 1999, © Greg Barrett, courtesy of Josef Lebovic Gallery, Sydney
Cover design: Daniel New
Typesetting: Megan Ellis
Editing: Meaghan Amor
Printed and bound in Australia by Griffin Press, part of Ovato

FSC® is dedicated to the promotion of responsible forest management worldwide. This book is made of material from FSC®-certified forests and other controlled sources.

Contents

PROLOGUE

Ballet boy lost

I was nineteen, a third-year student at The Australian Ballet School, burning with ambition and utterly obsessed with ballet. Cast in a coming-of-age story, I found myself transformed. Life was imitating art indeed.

Beyond Twelve is the story of a young boy's journey from football to ballet, and it has key roles for three male dancers. It was my opportunity of a lifetime, a chance to dance alongside two of The Australian Ballet's leading dancers, even though I wasn't yet officially in the company. The star of the cast was Kelvin Coe, the company's leading male dancer, around whom Graeme Murphy had, at least in part, choreographed the ballet to showcase his extraordinary talents. *Beyond Twelve* had premiered three years earlier in 1980 to great success, consolidating Murphy's long and illustrious choreographic relationship with The Australian Ballet.

The other leading dancers were Paul de Masson and Mark Annear, who had the role of the young boy. I was Mark's understudy and that age-old showbiz story played out as he suffered an injury during rehearsals. Suddenly, I had my chance not only to dance with the company I'd been dreaming about since I pulled on a pair of black jiffies at the age of seven, but to do so alongside my idol, Kelvin. We even joked we had been put in the same cast because of our noses: we were the 'big-nose cast'. I had always been self-conscious about the shape and size of my nose, but Kelvin and Paul had equally healthy proboscises, and we were about to dance together in a much-loved ballet. I was elated.

The company was slowly regrouping after a tumultuous couple of years. A seismic dancers' strike in 1981 had laid bare the artists' discontent about repertoire, standard and management. Kelvin, calm and articulate, became a reluctant spokesperson for the dancers. Many of the most senior dancers left the company, including Kelvin. For an ambitious young dancer, this state of affairs was a mixed bag: on the one hand, I was genuinely afraid for the future of the company I had loved since I was a child. But on the other hand, the resignations created opportunities for some graduate dancers from the school, like me and Steven Heathcote, to fill vacancies over the next few years and dance with the company. We unashamedly seized them.

After the initial fury had subsided and the dancers returned to work, Maina Gielgud was appointed artistic director; the company's CEO, Peter Bahen, left; and Kelvin returned as a guest artist to perform ballets such as *Beyond Twelve*. That was how I, a naive boy from Perth, landed a dancing role alongside Kelvin.

There are moments in ballet when you take a risk, when you try a difficult step or even make up one of your own. It's often a spontaneous thing, a rush of blood or bravado, but there is that millisecond in the air when you don't know if you're going to pull it off: it could be brilliant; it could be a disaster. Ballet asks you to engage with the unknown. And this period was inviting me to take that same risk.

Kelvin had been there, alongside me in some form, the whole time I'd been learning to dance. When I had been studying ballet for only a couple of years, my grandmother took me to see the company perform Frederick Ashton's *Cinderella* in a matinee at His Majesty's Theatre in Perth, and Kelvin, with his distinctive if not classically handsome features and his curly hair, had danced the lead with the wonderful Lucette Aldous. I was eight, already deeply in love with ballet and being mercilessly bullied about it at school. But on that day, I was so completely transported that when the performance ended and the doors opened, allowing the light to flood in from Hay Street, I got a huge shock because I'd completely forgotten where I was.

From then on, I read and watched everything I could about Kelvin. The next year, he and Marilyn Rowe won a silver medal at the prestigious Moscow International Ballet Competition, and my mum's *Women's Weekly* magazines often made mention of them – in the era of Rudolf Nureyev and Margot Fonteyn, ballet dancers could be superstars. I would grab these issues from her as soon as I could, devouring everything about the dancers, and especially Kelvin.

Then our paths crossed in an oh-so-peripheral way. I finally made it to Melbourne and The Australian Ballet School, which shared rehearsal space with the company at its Flemington studios. The Australian Ballet had been touring and we students had had the place to ourselves. One morning I was blithely walking down the corridor with a friend, unaware that the company had returned the night before. Kelvin rounded a corner ahead of us, just metres away from me. 'Oh my god, that's Kelvin Coe!' I blurted, which made Kelvin turn to look at me as if to say *Do I know you?* I was mortified by my outburst, and so I jumped into the nearest ballet studio, dying of embarrassment at my total lack of cool. To say that I was starstruck by Kelvin is something of an understatement.

A couple of years later, there I was rehearsing beside him. Mercifully by that time I was able to be in the same room as him without freaking out and wanting to hide. He was always kind and helpful, giving me pointers about how to do things better: 'You really need to work on this part,' he'd say, and show me how it was done.

After our performances in Sydney, he'd say to me, 'There's a group of us going to supper, would you like to come?'

'Great,' I'd reply, relishing any chance to spend even more time thinking and talking about ballet with people who also liked nothing more than thinking and talking about ballet. These were often large groups of dancers, so I didn't feel like he was singling me out for any special treatment.

Back in Melbourne, our friendship continued. I knew Kelvin was gay, but I had no idea what I was. I guess I probably suspected that I might have been, too, but I didn't want to be. After years and years of being called a 'poofter' and a 'pansy' at my all-boys Catholic school, I didn't want those bullies to be right. I dealt with it the same way I dealt with most things – pushing it to the back of my mind and focusing on ballet instead, determined to work harder than I had ever worked before.

In September that year, Kelvin had a birthday lunch at his big house in Healesville, a beautiful town about 60 kilometres north-east of Melbourne that is famous for its wildlife sanctuary. He had invited me, my dear friend Lizzie Toohey and his friend Cindy Sharp, and we all had a wonderful time. I thought nothing of it, until Paul de Masson threw a party for Kelvin at the house he shared with the ballet's conductor, Ormsby Wilkins, in the inner-city suburb of North Fitzroy.

Kelvin invited me and I gladly accepted, but when I arrived, the room was full of principals and soloists – and in those days, the company's ranks rarely mixed. I was a junior dancer in the corps de ballet and completely overwhelmed, surrounded by all these amazing dancers I admired. Suddenly, I felt crushingly shy. It was one of the most excruciating evenings of my life. But this was also when it dawned on me that Kelvin was introducing me to his group. All the senior dancers were looking at me with great interest, the *Ooooh, Kelvin's got a new friend* look etched all over their faces. I finally got it.

My friendship with Kelvin continued to develop; we saw a couple of movies together, but nothing more. Then, when we were on tour in Brisbane – staying in dreadful accommodation – things moved further. With our relationship changing, I found myself thinking more about whether I was, in fact, gay, even if I didn't want to be. Most of my closest friends in the company were gay men, and I felt safe with them. But I was still deeply conflicted.

One night during that Brisbane season, Kelvin asked me to dinner, which was not unusual – we would often have a meal together. But at the end of the meal he asked, 'Do you want to come up for a drink?' As a 'guest artist' he was staying in a rather posh hotel, in contrast to my impoverished share flat. I was elated to be asked up to his room, but even I knew what that meant. Both terrified and excited, I said to myself: *Deep breath, see what happens.*

Upstairs, we started kissing, then exploring each other, but my brain was struggling to simply enjoy the moment. *Oh my god, this is amazing!* I thought, followed by *Oh my god, what am I doing?* That night, Kelvin became my first lover. I didn't stay the night – I took my addled brain and rushed home, ecstatic from this experience but also still deeply troubled by what it all meant.

Over the next few months, I managed to compartmentalise these happy developments in my life in a very Catholic way: *As long as no one knows about it*, I thought, *it's okay*. Plus, I had discovered the joys of sex, and I kept looking forward to making love with this kind, gentle, caring man. But after several months of seeing each other regularly but secretly – he was often touring and so we would have imposed breaks – Kelvin indicated he wanted more. He was looking for a relationship, and a public one.

I was turning twenty and he was thirty-seven, so the gap in age and life experience between us seemed huge. Not that I ever felt there was an imbalance of power. Kelvin was a star and my idol, but he certainly never used this in any way to manipulate me in our relationship; quite the opposite, I was completely flattered and delighted by his interest. I was not a mature nineteen-year-old, and I had taken a fancy to making myself a bit of an enigma within the company, cultivating an air of mystery. Although I was enjoying our clandestine trysts, I was not prepared for our relationship to become public – I was not ready to come to terms with my sexuality, and I was not ready to be *known*. I started to back away and put some distance between us. Kelvin naturally noticed.

One evening when we were together, he made me do what I had been avoiding: talk about it. 'This relationship of ours,' he said, 'what are we doing here?'

I prevaricated. 'Well, I just don't know if I'm really up for being that committed,' I eventually replied.

He listened and paused, and then in his kind way – Kelvin was always kind – he let me off the hook. 'That's fine,' he said. 'You need to decide what you want to do. This isn't something I can decide for you.

You need to go away and work out what you want, and either I'll be here or someone else will.'

And that was it. Unable to deal with who I was, I pushed Kelvin away and shut myself off. At the time I was relieved to put aside the question that weighed on me so heavily. Kelvin and I remained friends – and occasional lovers – and he never once made me feel bad about the difficulty I had dealing with my sexuality, even when I had relationships with women.

And, of course, he was right – I needed to sort myself out. It would take me years to do so.

CHAPTER 1

Gotta dance

Television was my obsession when I was a very young boy, but only when it was turned off. My family proudly owned one of those solid wood sets, common in the 60s, that took up significant space in the lounge room.

Some shows interested me. Still not at school, I would wait excitedly for the clock to strike nine so I could watch *Play School* and join Lorraine Bayly and Alister Smart, my two favourite presenters, in their singing and dancing segments.

But the real reason I loved our big television was the discovery that, switched off, it was a very serviceable mirror that enabled me to watch myself dancing around the lounge room. Even better was when Mum had the radio switched on to classical music on the ABC. I could then pretend I was dancing for a (no doubt appreciative) audience. It was transporting.

Most adults can trace back elements of their adult selves to their childhoods, and that is certainly true for me. It seems from the time I took my first breath on 26 November 1963, I was obsessed with performing and determined to draw attention to myself at every opportunity. To say that made me unusual in my family – and in 1960s suburban Perth more generally – is a bit of an understatement.

Leaving aside the image of my small self gripped by my dancing reflection, ours was in many ways a typical Australian family of the time. My mum, Olive, and my dad, Don, had started dating when they were fourteen and sixteen respectively. Both had left school after their Junior Certificate (year 10) and had taken jobs at the Bank of New South Wales. They had fallen in love over their respective bank duties and, after several years of courtship, were married at St Mary's Catholic Church in Leederville, Perth.

It was a 'mixed' marriage, which at the time was considered an issue: Mum's family was staunchly Catholic; Dad's was, by default, Anglican. This had caused friction early on, as Dad's family wasn't too keen on him going steady with a Catholic girl, and Mum's preferred that she saw a nice Catholic boy. It was a case of history repeating, as Mum's mother had weathered a storm when she chose to marry my grandfather, who was also not a Catholic. I guess it was a case of like mother, like daughter!

Mum's mother was very serious about her Catholicism and had also had her share of tragedy. Mum's father, Travis, had had rheumatic fever as a child, which had permanently damaged a heart valve and left him significantly weakened. He had wanted to serve in the Second World War but his poor health meant he didn't pass the medical, and so he had become a milkman and then an ice delivery man. Mum's mum, known to us as 'Granny', was born in Kalgoorlie, about 600 kilometres east of Perth, into a large and prominent local family. But life for her and Travis was hard – after their marriage they moved from Kalgoorlie to a farm near where Mum was born. Despite working extremely hard, at one point they had to walk off their property because the land had become too saline to farm. I remember Mum telling the story of Granny and Grandpa leaving with a sixpence in their pockets. They had two children, my mum and her brother, Graeme, and as was the norm, Granny relied a great deal on my mum from a young age to help around the house.

Mum was a very bright girl, good at school, but was given few opportunities to do much with her intellect, as the expectation for girls, even the very clever ones, was to marry and have children – a desire Mum had dutifully adopted. Much later, Mum overheard Granny talking to her sister on the phone saying: 'Aren't we lucky we had daughters to look after us in our old age?' That irritated her intensely, not because of any deeply held feminist beliefs, but because it laid bare the inequity between sons and daughters: her brother had been the golden child in the family, whereas her role had been all about duty and responsibility. Olive was a wonderful mum, but who knows what she might have done if she had been born at a different time.

Travis's damaged heart finally gave out and he died tragically young, in his forties, just after Mum turned twenty-one and a year before she and Dad married. Granny never remarried and remained close to our family for the rest of her life – she would also become, somewhat unexpectedly, one of my great supporters in learning ballet. She visited us every Thursday, bringing lollies and pocket money. She also rang Mum every morning and was very miffed if Mum didn't pick up right on the dot of 9 am. Heaven forbid that the phone was engaged when she made her daily call!

Dad's parents, Nan and Pop, were also a big part of our lives when we were kids. Pop was a smart guy and worked in the insurance industry. He was also a champion whistler – we always knew they had arrived for a visit because we'd hear Pop's cheerful whistles as he walked around from the driveway to the back door.

Nan was a slightly discontented figure; she was born and raised in England, her own dad had been killed in the First World War, and her mother, with five kids in tow, had emigrated to Australia after the war. I got the sense that Nan thought she deserved more out of life, and at times was cranky as a result. Pop, who had severe asthma as an adult, retired from work at sixty-two, and died from the disease two years later. Dad was their only child, which was a huge burden on him. There was great pressure to meet his parents', and especially Nan's, ambitions. And one of the things she definitely didn't want him to be was Catholic. But Nan had to live with that disappointment: the church insisted before my parents were married that any children they had would be raised Catholic. Dad, in the spirit of 'if you can't beat 'em, join 'em', eventually decided it was easiest to convert.

Mum worked for a couple of years after she was married, but as soon as she became pregnant she left the bank to focus on being a wife and a mother. Dad studied to be an accountant, while still working, and for the rest of his career used his accounting skills in organisations with a social justice bent: he worked for St John Ambulance and later the Perth Catholic Archdiocese.

Neither of my parents were tall, and so I was destined to be short. Mum was only 157 centimetres tall, with olive skin, hazel eyes and dark hair. She also had a very distinctive square jawline that I inherited. The famous nose was also from Mum's side of the family, although she had somehow managed to avoid it (you can definitely see the origins of my aquiline nose in photos of her ancestors). My legs, especially my calves and hips, which I worried were too big for my entire dance career, were also handed down from my mum. Despite my concerns, I must admit the calves did come in handy helping to propel me into the air. Early in married life, Mum had worn a head of curls courtesy of the rollers she used to set her hair every night. But as the years went on and more children arrived, she replaced this hairstyle with a Mia Farrow–inspired pixie cut that had become very fashionable and which she pulled off extremely well.

At 172 centimetres, Dad was also slight, with fair skin, brown eyes and dark, wavy hair. He was a sporty kid who played a lot of tennis and remained fit throughout his life. Sadly, I didn't inherit his broad shoulders and slim hips – I also lacked his hand-eye coordination and ability to be handy around the house.

Two years after my parents were married, my brother Phillip was born, in August 1959. He was followed by my sister, Dianne, in December 1961, and then me in November 1963. Two years later, and much to my annoyance, my younger brother Paul arrived, stealing some of my limelight. It was another eight years before James arrived as a last-minute bundle of joy. Except for Phil, we were all born at the end of the year, and we always joked that we were conceived during Lent (our thinking was that our parents must have given up other things).

Mum and Dad bought a block of land in Woodlands, a northern suburb of Perth, and built a three-bedroom pale brick house on it, which meant all the boys had to share a bedroom. As the only girl, Di was allowed to have her own room. Later, when Phil was a teenager and James had arrived, Phil moved out, courtesy of an extension, and had his own bedroom. Paul, James and I shared the 'boys' room' – a space so big it was almost a dormitory – until I left home at seventeen. Mine was the middle of the three beds, neatly lined up and each decked out in matching green chenille bedspreads that were upgraded to a very on-trend gold and teal floral in the 1970s. Underneath each were cotton sheets in the summer, and flannelette sheets with blankets in the winter. Sunday was washing day and, in keeping with my mother's love of strict routine, every washing day we were given a clean bottom sheet; the previous week's bottom sheet became the top sheet, and the old top sheet and pillowcase went to the laundry.

Underneath our beds were drawers that housed our toys and personal things that were special to us – in mine was my beloved Fuzzy-Felt kit, toys and picture books. Above my bed was a cross Granny had given me. My greatest treasure was housed in the room's communal chest of drawers: a collection of ballet books.

While the house itself was fairly cosy, the backyard was huge. There was a patio where we often had parties or ate dinner (especially on hot nights). In a familiar Australian scene, the big yard was punctuated by a Hills hoist. If we ever complained of being bored, Mum shooed us into the backyard where we built cubbies and exhausted ourselves running around. If we were really lucky, Mum would succumb to our badgering on summer days and take us to see Aunty Betty and Uncle Bert, who had that most coveted thing: a swimming pool. Even though we lived quite close to the beach, we rarely visited it, but going to Aunty Betty and Uncle Bert's house for a swim was always a cause for immense excitement. We eventually got our own pool in 1973, about the same time as our youngest brother, James, arrived. I would spend so long in the water that most days I ended up wrinkled like a sultana, and every summer I sported a tan that rivalled the most committed sun-worshipper. Sometimes, on oppressively hot Perth nights, we'd be allowed to go for a swim at night, and we'd happily drift off to sleep with the smell of chlorine on our skin.

The extension that enabled Phil to have his own room also brought another delight: French doors that were framed in teal curtains, opening out from the kitchen onto the patio. In my mind this created an ideal performance space. I used to love dramatically parting the drapes to deliver a show on the patio. At one point Nan had plastic runners put down in her new flat that were delivered wrapped in thick paper for protection. I collected all the wrapping paper and used it to create framing borders to transform the patio into a stage. It didn't last long, though, as they were only held up with sticky tape – my career was never going to be in stage design.

Ours was a very happy childhood, but that didn't stop me from being a handful. Theatrical, stubborn and given to tantrums, I was often in trouble. My parents had a 'naughty boys' stick' that was kept on top of the kitchen cupboards, and I'm pretty sure I was the only one it was ever used on. If I were a child now, my parents would probably be hauling me off to specialists for diagnosis, but at the time I was simply referred to as 'spirited', accompanied by a pained expression from all who had to endure my antics. I was restless, fidgety and easily bored – constant reprimands always began with: 'If you don't sit still, David ...'

I twigged pretty early on that being obnoxious was a way to get attention, and so I put a lot of energy into it. When I was two, my aunt was getting married, and Phil and Di had been given the jobs of ring bearer and flower girl. I was beside myself with jealousy that they were performing and I wasn't, and I threw an almighty tantrum at the wedding. Pop, in an effort to calm me, suggested I lie down under his chair, where I duly fell asleep.

When Paul arrived two years after me, I really upped the ante. I had lost my precious position as the youngest child; Phil was the oldest, Di was the only girl, and now Paul was the youngest, and I suddenly became, in my view, remarkably ordinary, a forgotten – possibly even a tragic – figure. I was determined to be the notorious middle child. Soon after, at Pop's sixtieth birthday celebration, I regaled everyone with my first public dance performance. Colourful globes had been festooned around Pop and Nan's backyard, and people were making their way to and from a huge keg of beer for refills. My grandparents also had a septic tank in their backyard that, to me, was the perfect stage: round, elevated, attention-grabbing. Nan had a portable record-player with speakers attached that was playing an array of *Reader's Digest* classics such as 'Kitten on the Keys'. I decided this was my moment to shine, so I jumped on the septic tank and danced my heart out. All the guests thought it was adorable for the first ten minutes, but as the performance neared the one-hour mark I was sent inside to bed, with a stern instruction not to even think about an encore.

As well as being theatrical, I was stubborn. It was a trait that must have tried my parents' patience immensely but would come in handy later in life. I recall one time I was in trouble – I cannot remember precisely what for now – and my father asked me to apologise to my mother. I refused, so I was smacked. 'Apologise to your mother,' he insisted. Again I refused, and again I was smacked, which made me all the more determined not to apologise. On and on we went, my father's frustration rising and my heels digging in further each time. Where would this end? Eventually, my poor dad could see that it was a lost cause and walked out. Later, I realised I had been wrong and apologised to my mother, and everything was forgiven. My dad still tells this story to this day – the trials of parenting a wilful child.

I was only too happy to have a grand-scale meltdown – *the drama!* – and I literally threw my whole body into it, often to the point where my parents became concerned I would hurt myself. I would slide to the floor, or leap into the air and throw myself down for maximum effect, shrieking at the same time. Later, my younger brother Paul would try to emulate my tantrum-throwing but, afraid of hurting himself, would only attempt the dramatic body slam onto a carefully placed cushion.

Dancing and performing came as naturally to me as breathing. As a kid I had been given Matchbox cars and trucks to play with, but they held little interest for me. I was far more absorbed with my sister's dolls and the Fuzzy-Felt kits containing cut-out felt shapes that were placed on a felt board to create themed pictures. I had the circus Fuzzy-Felt but Di had the ballet kit that I desperately wanted, and when she eventually lost interest in it and gave it to me, I was euphoric.

I also loved escaping into a fantasy world of make-believe. I had a well-stocked dress-up box that fuelled many of these adventures. It was mainly made up of Mum's and Granny's old dresses and shoes and anything that could be turned into a costume. Di and I were the regular cast members of these theatrical exploits, but sometimes we enlisted other members of the family. Many times it was a solo escapade, which could take hours to develop and enjoy; often I became disillusioned when I was told to 'get out of all that garb' or when my desire to put on a show to present my latest folly was very quickly dismissed in preference to serving the evening meal. The capacity of children to fantasise is an amazing and precious ability. It enables them to fully believe that their bed is a car taking them on a journey without leaving their bedroom, or that an old discarded Osti frock is a fairy queen's ball gown. It can even transform a pair of pointy-toed 'champagne'-heeled stilettoes into high fashion 70s wedgies with some discarded jarrah offcuts, a buzz saw and some Aquadhere industrial wood glue.

I was also always drawing, particularly brides. I was obsessed with weddings. I loved the theatricality of them, the beauty and romance of the dresses, the whole spectacle of the event. Later, when I was an altar boy at church, weddings were my favourite service to be part of, not only because we got $5 per wedding – a huge sum at the time – but so I could critique the bride's entrance, the drama level, the overall performance. My uncle Graeme was a butcher, and so we were supplied with huge pads of butcher's paper to draw on, which I filled with pictures of brides. As part of a large Catholic family, we attended lots of weddings, where I was completely fixated on what the bride was wearing and the entrance she made. Moreover, there was an Italian family living across the street from us who seemed to go to a wedding just about every week. I would sit with my sister, Di – the sibling to whom I was always closest – and watch them come out of the house on their way to a wedding, loving all the bright-coloured dresses and the ladies' hair styled into incredible bouffants.

I can honestly say that I have no idea where I inherited my love of performing. No one in my family showed the slightest interest in ballet. My dad's Aunty Jean was an opera singer, and quite a good one – she had recorded a '78' that we used to play on Granny's wind-up record-player. Looking back she had a very strong voice, influenced by the great divas of the past, with a vibrato that made the room quaver. Aunty Jean later claimed she was the source of my talent, but the truth is my love of performing – and my absolute obsession with ballet – was a bolt out of the blue.

Mum was a no-nonsense but extremely loving mother. She was also a deft hand with the sewing machine. She made most of her own clothes as well as most of ours, and I loved it when the black Singer came out of the cupboard and she'd start cutting material for a new dress. I used to sit and watch her work all day, and she often gave me the scraps that I'd then use to make dresses for Di's dolls or turn into something creative for my own enjoyment.

Her other important job was to manage the household budget. And she did it well. My dad would come home and hand her his pay packet, and she would immediately divide up the cash – a bit here for bills, a bit here for groceries, a bit here for new clothes and shoes. We were not wealthy by any stretch of the imagination, but we also never went without anything – our parents made sure of that.

In the afternoons we would have a 'nap', when we were sent to our bedrooms to be quiet for an hour. I think my mum just needed a rest herself, and so we were dispatched to our beds with a book, even before I could read. We'd wait a while and then start asking 'Can we get up yet?' from our bedrooms, which was inevitably met with a firm 'No' until the hour was up.

At night, when it was time for bed, Mum would come into the boys' room and kiss each of us goodnight. One of the smells I have always associated with her is Oil of Ulan, which she used to moisturise her face and neck; its scent would drift into my nostrils as she gave her goodnight kiss. She used it all her life, and later I would moisturise with it after removing my stage make-up – a habit I've maintained to this day. After she died, the connection between that smell and my memory of her became even more powerful, and it still fills me with feelings of calm and security.

Mum's menu for the week followed a strict formula. Meals were allocated to specific days of the week, a routine that was rarely deviated from: sausages on Monday, a roast midweek, fish and chips on Friday (a personal highlight) and so it went on. In hindsight, I have a lot of sympathy for my mum in those days, because so much of what she did was performance, too: usually with a far less appreciative audience. The house was always spotless in case we had visitors; there needed to be cake in the tin and neat and tidy children. When visitors did arrive, we all had to behave ourselves and conform to the old adage of 'being seen but not heard' as well as the more important 'family hold back' to ensure we didn't make 'piggies' of ourselves by scoffing all the food.

Going to church was an important part of the family routine. We all had to go, and we had to wear our 'Sunday best' – there were hats, gloves and ties as far as the eye could see. Dad, the Catholic convert, had embraced his new denomination wholeheartedly. He had also embraced being a lad wholeheartedly, especially in the early years of family life, and enjoyed occasionally going out drinking with his mates. I have a strong memory of going to midnight Mass on Christmas Eve and my dad, a little worse for wear, falling asleep during the service.

In keeping with my Troubled Middle Child persona, I was a handful at church. Sitting still for a long time was a special kind of torture – I was the kid often seen screaming during the service or being dragged out by his embarrassed parents. Later, when I had started at Catholic school and had begun to learn ballet, Phil became an altar boy. This led me to realise that there was an opportunity to actually *perform* in church rather than just endure it, so of course I was keen to join up as well, and I loved having the eyes of the congregation on me.

Part of the attraction was the costume. When I first became an altar boy, the uniform was a white soutane – an ankle-length religious dress – with a lovely lacy top over it. But soon after they changed the uniform and the new one had a distinctly 1970s vibe – very straight and plain with a hood at the back and a black belt that dropped down. One gratifying aspect of it, though, was that the soutane was short enough to reveal my David Bowie–esque bulb-toe platform shoes, of which I was immensely proud. Aspiring to be a cool teenager, it was all about the show.

As a younger child, I went through a phase of being quite religious – the pomp and ceremony drew me in. My devout granny, whom I loved very much, used to give us holy cards and books about saints for our birthdays. I was very taken with the stories of the saints – *so much drama, yet so much triumph!* – and briefly entertained a fantasy of becoming one. That was soon struck down by reality, however, especially when I discovered there was no patron saint of ballet.

Most kids look forward to going to school, but not me. Having only just turned five in November the year before, there was some discussion about whether to hold me back for another year. But my parents eventually decided, given my precocious nature, that my attention-seeking was a sign that I needed greater stimulation, so I was signed up for Our Lady of the Rosary Primary School, where Phil had been and Di attended.

I was devastated. I could see that school brought with it the complete annihilation of the fantasy world I had built up around me and would replace it with a world of rules and duty. On my first day, in the baking hot Perth heat, I was packed off in my grey school uniform to begin grade 1 (there was no prep or kindergarten in those days), tagging behind my only safety net, my sister, who was heading into grade 3. Let's just say the induction was brisk. The nuns led us in and that was it – we were left alone to figure it out ourselves.

I was tiny, even for five, and surrounded by kids I didn't know and, worse still, didn't know me. I had become invisible – my greatest fear. I had no friends and had been dropped in an alien environment full of rules I didn't understand, or didn't want to understand. I had no time to escape into my fantasy world, where I felt safe, loved and appreciated, where I was the star of the show. By the time the lunchbreak arrived, I was walking around the playground in tears, feeling trapped and, in typical fashion, responding to my feelings with intense melodrama. Di was the only person who would talk to me and was something of a saviour in those days, though understandably she soon became sick of her little brother following her everywhere and insisted I make my own friends.

I spent my early days at primary school in a fog of misery. I wasn't particularly interested in learning, and I struggled with reading all through my schooling. I was small, skinny and lonely, and I only really came alive in the creative subjects such as art or music – a program on ABC radio called *Let's Join In* was a favourite, as we got to sing along with all the songs, following the lyrics in books we were given. It was probably the only time I enjoyed reading.

One day in grade 1, I was miserable with a terrible pain in my ear. It was so bad that I put my head on the desk and cried, until my kindly teacher, Mrs Jarret, remembered that my Aunty Betty was volunteering in the school tuckshop that day, so she took me over to her and said, 'I think you'd better do something with David.' Aunty Betty's remedy made me exceedingly happy: she sat me next to the pie-warmer and gave me a burnt pastie they couldn't sell in the tuckshop, letting me sit there while they finished the clean-up from lunch, munching away. By the time she took me home I had pus leaking from my ear, and a trip to the doctor revealed an abscess that had burst. Sure, my ear was sore, but I was headed for a few more days off school, tucked up on the grey woollen lounge chair with a pillow and blanket, watching television on my own. I was in heaven.

Soon after this event, something unexpectedly pleasant happened at school. I was wandering around in my usual gloom one lunchtime when I saw a young boy my age making a cubbyhouse out of rocks and gumnuts. I stopped and watched for a while and then, once I was satisfied that he was harmless, began collecting gumnuts and offering them to him. 'Can I play with you?' I ventured nervously, bracing for rejection. But Tim Foley was also somewhat of an outsider, shy and sensitive. He looked up and said, 'Sure,' and my heart flipped with joy. Tim and I started building the cubby together; from that day, we remained firm friends all through our schooling. Along with Di, Tim was my greatest ally and friend, especially when school became brutal.

On the surface, Tim and I were something of an odd couple. He was tall with strawberry blond hair and blue eyes; I was short and dark. A growth spurt eventually saw Tim shoot up to 190 centimetres while I was a full 30 centimetres shorter. In later years I often stood on the brick fence surrounding the school garden bed so we could talk face to face. But apart from our looks, we had much in common: both of us were hopeless at sport and preferred art – we often stayed in the art room during lunchtime, working on a project. We spent most of our time together, along with a few other boys who preferred more artistic pursuits to the sports culture that permeated the school.

My deep desire to perform had not been shaken by school, and I still escaped into my fantasy world – in which I was always on stage – at every opportunity. My eye for performance remained sharp. Our head nun at school, Sister Dominica – a fearsome woman – was having an anniversary of some sort: thirty or perhaps forty years as a nun. These were the sorts of celebrations that brought a great deal of excitement at Catholic school, and I was particularly interested in the 'spiritual bouquet' we were all contributing to in order to mark the occasion. I imagined an arrangement of flowers in every colour of the rainbow, so big Sister Dominica would barely be able to hold it. When it arrived, though, it was bits of felt stuck onto some kind of hessian poster and surrounded by a collection of Hail Marys that people had contributed. I remember being completely crushed by this sight.

The following year, with Tim Foley still mercifully by my side, I was taken from the calm and kind domain of Mrs Jarret and into the grade 2 class of Mrs Buegge, an altogether different proposition. Mrs Buegge was groovy, a paragon of late 60s Mary Quant–style fashion, with a short Vidal Sassoon hairstyle that sat up at the back and flattened into sharp edges around her face. I thought she was the most beautiful woman I had ever seen. She wore micro-minis – so micro, in fact, that when she bent over we could see her underwear, to our great excitement – and suede boots. In the afternoon, if we were tired, we'd sit on a square of carpet at her feet stroking her long suede boots while she read to us. Nowadays, kids stroking their teacher's legs would probably be discouraged, but in those days no one thought anything of it. She was so glamorous, I was completely enchanted. I learnt very little that year.

My standout performance at school that year – apart from being told off during religious classes for plaiting Karen McCarthy's hair instead of thinking about God – came on Anzac Day. There was to be a special Mass to honour the fallen on Anzac Day, and the teachers asked if any of us had fathers or grandfathers who had died in the war. I knew that my mum's dad was dead and, sensing a theatrical opportunity, shot up my hand. I was chosen to take the flowers to the altar in front of the whole school, which I relished. Later, I proudly told my mum about this. 'I was chosen because Grandpa died in the war,' I boasted. 'No, he didn't,' was my mother's slightly mortified response, which I think somewhere in the back of my mind I knew, but still – never let an opportunity go by. I was that sort of kid.

When would I get my chance to finally perform and learn to dance? Every approach I had made to my parents had been rebuffed. Despite me constantly prancing around the living room and tap dancing on the septic tank, as well as putting together endless performances on the patio, they still saw my interest in dancing as a childish fancy that would pass. In their world, little boys didn't learn ballet – not that they were particularly against it, but it was simply way outside of their orbit. A theatrical child was amusing – occasionally embarrassing – and an interest in performance not something that needed to be acted on, or encouraged. My constant badgering of 'I want to learn ballet, I want to learn ballet' had been gently dismissed with a 'too hard' kind of response and the fervent wish that I would grow out of it, hopefully soon.

But in the 1960s, ballet was unexpectedly and consistently in international headlines thanks to one dancer: Rudolf Nureyev. Born on a train in Siberia, in the Soviet Union, Nureyev was supremely gifted and attracted notice from a young age; he rose to become a principal dancer with the famed Kirov Ballet and was a sensation in the Soviet Union. Despite efforts by the KGB to stop him, he famously defected to the West in 1961, an event that attracted attention around the world.

Soon after, he danced with the fledgling Australian Ballet (which had evolved from the Borovansky company in 1962). He built a close rapport with the company from that first visit in 1964 when, accompanied by his equally famous dance partner, British ballerina Margot Fonteyn, he had been greeted like a movie star. Handsome (his cheekbones looked like they would burst through his skin), sexy and charismatic, Nureyev could be fiery and difficult, and generous and charming. The press couldn't get enough of him, especially with the speculation that he and Fonteyn were a couple off stage as well as on.

In 1966, Nureyev staged his own version of *Don Quixote* for the Vienna State Opera, and in 1970, to great fanfare, he brought it to The Australian Ballet. Later, in 1972, he offered the dancers of the young company an even more exciting opportunity: performing in a film version of the ballet, with Nureyev and Lucette Aldous as its stars and under Nureyev's and Sir Robert Helpmann's direction (Helpmann played the Don). The film was made over a summer in a stiflingly hot aeroplane hangar at Essendon Airport, with Nureyev, ever the perfectionist, often keeping the dancers late into the night until he was happy with a scene.

Perhaps the most significant ballet dancer of the 20th century, Nureyev changed the art form forever. One of the ways he did that was to revolutionise the role of the male dancer in ballet: no longer just a prop to support the ballerina, a male dancer could come to the forefront and be a star in his own right.

But all of that was to come later. In 1970, he had arrived in Australia to perform, and everyone knew about it. One evening, my family was gathered in front of our television when a mini-documentary came on to Channel 7, largely to promote the season of *Don Quixote* that featured Nureyev, with Aldous as Kitri. That a ballet could command a peak-hour timeslot on commercial television gives you some indication of what a huge star Nureyev was. The doco showed an abridged version of *Don Quixote*, featuring the Seguidilla dance in Act I. It was probably from a dress rehearsal, with a bit of Nureyev shown and then a snippet of him and Aldous dancing the grand pas de deux. For a child who had just turned seven, it was like a bolt of lightning had struck. I was completely mesmerised by this man and the things he could do. *A man can dance like that?*

The leaps, the turns, the charisma, the theatricality – I wanted it all. I wanted to be Nureyev, to dance with a guitar, lift a beautiful girl into the air, leap and turn around the stage – at the same time! – move to that stirring music, bring the audience to its feet. All of my endless nagging of my parents – 'I want to learn ballet, I want to learn ballet' – which I had sustained for close to a year, was crystallised in that moment, and I knew it was the only place I belonged.

I turned to my parents once again as we watched this magnetic performance on the television and begged them: 'Please, I want to learn ballet!' And this time they realised the pestering wasn't going to stop. They, too, had been impressed by the way Nureyev danced, and they knew how famous he was. For the sake of their own peace as much as anything, they finally agreed.

It wasn't easy to find someone who would teach a boy ballet. In those days, and sadly still today, girls vastly outnumbered boys in ballet schools. Many of the teachers my parents approached said no, because taking on a boy meant learning a whole new syllabus to teach. My parents kept following leads, asking around. One day, I heard the postman's whistle and went outside. In the letterbox was something that made my heart race: an envelope with the stamp of a ballerina in arabesque on it. I ran inside.

'Mum, what's this, what's this?' I demanded.

Mum, in her calm way, took the envelope from me. 'Yes, we've enrolled you in a ballet class,' she said.

I can't remember what she said next, because I had drifted away. I was on cloud nine. Finally, *finally*, I would get to learn ballet. It was the end of the year and I had to wait three agonising months before I could start, but nonetheless, it was going to happen.

My parents still weren't convinced it would last. 'We'll just send him along, he'll probably hate it, and then it will all be over,' was their approach.

How wrong they were.

CHAPTER 2

Taking flight

Black jiffies. There they were: stiff, ill-fitting and definitely not what proper dancers wore – even at seven, I had studied ballet enough to know that. These were soft vinyl slippers with an elastic border mainly worn by girls, and although they were shaped like a ballet shoe, to my mind at least they did not have the allure or prestige of the 'real' thing. Yet my mother would not budge: she had, as requested, kitted me out in black football shorts and a white T-shirt from our local Coles variety store, but she was not about to splurge on a pair of kid leather ballet shoes for what was likely a passing fancy. Nothing could have encapsulated my parents' attitude to me learning ballet more succinctly than the jiffies – not hostile, just sceptical.

Despite my discontent about the footwear, my excitement was infinite. I put on my ballet outfit for every visitor to our house over the summer break, regaling them excitedly with details about my forthcoming beginners' class. Finally, one hot Saturday morning in February 1971, the big day arrived: Mum and Dad deposited me at the Progress Hall in Gildercliffe Street, Scarborough, for my first ballet lesson with Miss Evelyn Hodgkinson. It was a convention that female teachers were usually referred to as 'Miss (surname)' and these days, it is 'Miss (first name)', a nod to the art form's mannered, disciplined history. Teachers were called 'Miss' regardless of whether they were married – in ballet, everyone is young, or ought to be.

The hall was an old weatherboard building, slightly worse for wear, with a small porch out the front and a cork noticeboard where local businesses or charities posted news of upcoming events or pleas for donations. To one side was a modest kitchen with Arnott's biscuits, Nescafé instant coffee and Bushells tea bags in the cupboards, which were kept locked at the weekend to protect them from hungry children post-ballet classes.

As I poked my head around the door, I looked past the thirty young girls all staring at me and noticed, with delight, that there was a stage at one end of the hall, framed by a worn (but nonetheless wonderfully theatrical) red curtain that was pulled back to reveal a very magical space. From high windows, shafts of light beamed down on the wooden floor, highlighting little swirls of dust.

Then I noticed all the girls looking at me, a great curiosity – a boy who reckoned he was going to learn ballet – and, suddenly shy, I gripped my mother's hand tightly. Miss Hodgkinson was friendly but brisk: 'You must be David,' she said, approaching us with a smile. She seemed old to me – about the same age as my granny – with red hair that was turning grey and disciplined into a neat hairstyle with the help of nightly rollers. She was wearing a short-sleeved knitted jumper and a pleated, woollen plaid skirt that showed off a pair of shapely calves honed, I later discovered, by a career as a champion Highland dancer. Her voice was deep and gravelly, probably made more so from years of shouting at errant dancers, but her eyes sparkled with good humour. She was an impressive woman, warm but no-nonsense and, as it turned out, an excellent teacher.

Miss Hodgkinson did not allow parents to stay and watch the class, as it was too distracting for the young dancers. My mum was kindly shooed away and told to come back in an hour as I was absorbed into a sea of pink leotards and buns, Billy Elliot–style. The 'barre' in Miss Hodgkinson's class wasn't a barre at all, but stacks of metal chairs, three on top of each other, lined up with their backs facing into the hall. As the class began, I learnt a whole new vocabulary, starting with plié and *tendu*. Miss Hodgkinson demonstrated the step first, then made her way over to the reel-to-reel tape recorder – a massive piece of equipment – to play the recorded music.

The girls all seemed to know the steps, so I had to catch up, and I did so quickly. I remember noticing a lot of side eye from my classmates as they tried to get a grip on this alien in their midst and assess how long he might be planning to stay. But I didn't care. It was bliss – finally, I felt I belonged. Easily distracted at school, here I was a model of concentration, determined to learn all the steps and then perfect them.

After the barre exercises we moved to the centre of the hall, and in a rather strange version of the 'ladies first' convention, I was placed in the back row because I was a boy. After each exercise, the front row ran to the back and a new set of dancers had their time in the limelight. I approached the front line, when my turn finally came, with a mixture of trepidation and excitement. I was nervous about not yet knowing the steps – and there had been some comfort in being surrounded by all those girls who knew what they were doing – but I was also looking forward, in my signature style, to showing off under the teacher's gaze. The exercise at the front was a practice for the 'spotting' that is so important in turns. We had to focus on a point at the front of the classroom, then shuffle our feet around in a tight circle, leaving our eyes to the front for as long as possible and then quickly turning our heads and returning our eyes to the original spot. Miss Hodgkinson praised me for doing the exercise well and I was thrilled, by now deeply in love with the class and with having the opportunity to do 'real' ballet rather than my own version in front of the television.

Finally, we learnt how to do a *révérence* – a curtsy for the girls and a bow for me – before Miss Hodgkinson opened the door back out into the real world, where another noisy group of aspiring ballet dancers was waiting for their turn in the limelight. Miss Hodgkinson made a point of taking me to my mother herself. 'He did very well,' she told her. 'We look forward to seeing you next week.'

I was beaming with pride, and desperately wanted to show Mum and Dad – who was waiting for me in the car – what I had learnt. But it was Saturday morning, which meant wrangling our large brood for the chore of grocery shopping, so it would have to wait. As soon as I got in the car, Dad asked, 'How did it go?' and before I could answer, he added, 'You know you don't have to go back if you don't want to.' It was an offer he repeated every Saturday morning – perhaps in hope, perhaps just bewilderment – in the coming weeks. But eventually he stopped, as every Saturday I reported that the class was wonderful and I couldn't wait to go back.

The hall in Gildercliffe Street became the focal point of my life, and a source of abiding happiness. Gradually, I caught up to the girls in terms of familiarity with the steps, and my confidence and skills developed, too. One day, we were to learn the party polka, a staple of the Royal Academy of Dance syllabus. This British organisation was set up in 1920 to standardise the teaching of ballet and ensure a better quality of teaching via a staged syllabus through which one could train and progress by examinations, which were managed from London. It has become one of the most recognised providers of learning and support for ballet teaching and has accredited teachers around the globe.

The party polka involved dancing with a partner, one arm stretched out, holding hands, the other hand on each other's waists. Of course, none of the girls were particularly keen on dancing with the only boy. I was initially paired with a girl named Monique who, on hearing the news, burst into loud tears. But that was when a bubbly blonde girl named Louise stepped forward and said she would dance with me, not only relieving me of my humiliation, but also launching another of the most important friendships of my childhood.

Louise Ward was small and energetic, like me, with so much personality that she could light up the room when she was dancing. She was a terrific dancer, a kind person and lots of fun, and we hit it off immediately. The youngest of three girls, Louise, happily, lived quite close to me. From the day of the party polka, we became best friends. We often went to each other's houses to play, where we'd talk endlessly about how we'd get married when we grew up. And as I was obsessed with weddings and, at that stage, assumed I would only ever marry a girl, I was able to plan a happy future with Louise. The wedding would be grand, with the bridesmaids wearing lime green – remember, this was the 1970s – and we would live in a house with cane furniture and shag carpet (see reminder about it being the 70s). We also thought we'd have beanbags instead of a lounge suite.

After we'd imagined our wedding for the millionth time, we'd play an extended game of 'mothers and fathers' before it became dark and one of us had to head home.

Those blissful days with Louise would all come later, and in some ways would be a saving grace. But first, I was about to make a huge mistake at school, which haunted me for years. Riding high after my first ballet class, which was every bit as amazing as I had imagined it would be, I couldn't wait to get to school on Monday and share my happy news.

Every Monday morning we had 'news' in our classroom, where we were encouraged to tell any exciting experiences we'd had in the previous week. On this particular Monday, I fidgeted until the teacher asked for any volunteers to kick off the discussion. I shot up my hand, desperate to enlighten everyone with my news. When she finally called on me, I stood up and proudly announced: 'My news is that I went to ballet class on Saturday.' Expecting the usual polite, slightly indifferent applause, I was instead greeted with giggling and whispering behind hands. I was crushed – why weren't they all as excited about this as I was? By the time we were out in the playground for recess, the mood had shifted, and I realised I had made a major faux pas. I had never been terribly popular at school, but now I was a complete pariah, especially in the eyes of the boys.

It wasn't just the kids who found my new interest hard to accept, either. The fact that I was taking ballet classes filtered through to the staffroom and swiftly made its way up the grapevine to the head nun, Sister Dominica, who decided it was a matter of such gravity that she called my parents in for a discussion. 'Little boys don't learn ballet,' she informed them, and suggested that I be swiftly unenrolled from my classes.

While this could have frightened my parents, it actually only galvanised their support. My dad, in particular, bridled at being told how he should raise his child – he still retained some of his outsider's healthy scepticism towards the Catholic Church – and firmly replied: 'If my son wants to learn ballet, then he will, and no one is going to tell me that he can't.'

And so I did. Every Saturday morning, I was there at the hall, turning, stretching, jumping, bending and learning the strict, challenging, glorious technique of classical ballet. As time went on, Miss Hodgkinson decided that I should do the Royal Academy of Dance examinations, and that meant having private lessons to learn the boys' syllabus. In order to do this I had to finish school a little early on Wednesdays, and when I was very young, Granny collected me and took me on the bus to Gildercliffe Street for these classes. Granny had become a great ally in learning ballet – in her eyes, I could do no wrong. She was also given the rare privilege of being allowed to sit and watch the classes. Miss Hodgkinson and Granny had hit it off, both being from Kalgoorlie and around the same age, so Granny was treated differently from the mums and dads at the school.

Because I was, for so long, the only boy in the ballet school, I took all the exams on my own; the examiners who came to our school usually tested the students in pairs rather than in larger groups. I received honours in every year level. Years later, another boy called Alexander came to our ballet school, and we sometimes trained together. But he was much younger than I was, so I felt like more of a coach or mentor to him – although I'm not sure how much dance knowledge I had to impart at that stage.

As I continued with my dancing at Gildercliffe Street, Louise and I were presented with an amazing opportunity: we were to perform on stage with the Perth City Ballet in *The Nutcracker*. At the request of Diana Waldron, who was the artistic director of the company, we were both chosen by Miss Hodgkinson to be part of the cast of children and we were overcome with excitement: my first official performance, and this time, people actually wanted me to perform!

It really felt like we had hit the big time. The performances were at Perth Concert Hall, and the company had professional dancers, sets and costumes – Mum had been given a pattern and had sewn my costume. Dad dropped Louise and me off at the stage door and picked us up again when the performance ended. I have a very strong memory of him telling me off for not holding the stage door open for Louise to enter.

The first time we were to go on stage, I was suddenly struck by the idea of performing in front of so many people. Excited and terrified, I had a brief moment when I couldn't move, paralysed by all the big emotions coursing through my body. But, as quickly as it came, it passed, and I soon realised the ecstasy of being able to give myself completely to a performance, of becoming utterly lost in the story I was telling and the character I was portraying. That feeling has stayed with me throughout my life.

Perth City Ballet had some excellent dancers, and I was in awe of all of them. The leading couple was Kerry Wilson and Ken McSwain, and I remember being gobsmacked when, during the grand pas de deux, he did a toss flip into a 'fish dive', which entailed throwing his partner into the air, causing her to spin twice before landing in his arms in an arch, resembling a flying fish – I couldn't imagine ever being able to do that. There was also a beautiful young dancer called Nicole Pashley dancing the role of Clara – she had long auburn hair that she wore in curlers to rehearsals. I thought this was exceptionally glamorous.

At school, things were not nearly as happy. Already something of an outlier for being small and unsporty in a sports-mad school, I was also the 'ballerina', 'pansy' and now a new word: 'poofter'. I had no idea what this meant, but I knew it wasn't good. The boys who said it probably didn't know what it meant, either. But in those unenlightened days, to be like a 'girl' – and therefore not a 'proper' boy – was about as bad as it got, and my schoolmates threw those words at me with relish.

I eventually worked up the courage to ask my mum what a poofter was. She looked suitably concerned and said it 'wasn't nice', and that I should take no notice. If I ignored them, she advised, they would soon grow tired of calling me names and stop. If only it was that simple.

Instead, I became the class punching bag – during sports, in particular, the boys took any opportunity they could to trip or punch me, or hit me hard with the ball. Tunnel ball was an especially good opportunity to target me. My parents continued to support me as best they could, but they were not aware just how bad it had become. Mum's advice to ignore it was probably wise, as I wasn't in a position to fight back, and I didn't want to fight, anyway. When he arrived at primary school two years after me, at the height of my ballet-based infamy, my brother Paul copped a lot of flak as well. 'You're the poofter's brother,' they'd shout at him, and Paul was understandably resentful that he'd inherited notoriety from his dancing brother.

I did have some allies, though. Tim continued to be my great friend, and we had a few other mates who we kept close to (and, to their great credit, they were not deterred by my schoolyard disrepute).

The girls were generally kinder than the boys, and I felt much safer with them.

In grade 4, I had a lovely teacher named Mrs Firth. She noticed that I was being targeted, and so one day when I had left early to go to ballet, she instructed the bullies to be kinder to me. This, astonishingly, had the desired effect, and I was given a couple of days' grace from the incessant taunting. But then one lunchtime I was invited to play a game of 'kiss chasey' with my classmates on the oval, during which they all accused me of wanting to kiss the boys rather than the girls. At eight years old, such a thing had never crossed my mind (that came later), but the result was that I was swiftly returned to the centre of their scorn.

Other teachers were also kind. Even Sister Dominica, our stern head nun, came to the end-of-year concert the ballet school performed at Perth Town Hall. She was very impressed and admitted to my parents later that it was wonderful to see the rigour of my training and the fact I had obviously gained a great deal of confidence from learning ballet. She also thought I showed tremendous ability. From then on, Sister Dominica took more of an interest in my dance career, though she did always insist on mistakenly calling me 'Ian'. You can't have everything.

While there were pockets of relief from the bullying, it got a whole lot worse. Our Lady of the Holy Rosary Primary School was only co-educational until grade 4, so in 1973 I was enrolled in the all-boys Marist Brothers Junior School in Wembley. While this was in some ways a chance to make a fresh start – by this time I had sadly learnt not to be so open about learning ballet – it was not to be. On my first day at the new school, Mum took me to my new class, where I met the boy I was to sit next to, Michael. Mum decided he and I would be firm friends, which worked out very well on day one. But there was still a large group of boys who knew me from primary school and set about informing everyone of my 'poofter' status. I quickly became a focal point for the whole school, and not in a good way. Michael decided the pressure was too much and called off our fledgling friendship, telling me we were not to be seen together in the playground. Once again, I was left baffled. *I'm a nice person*, I reasoned, *so why don't they like me?*

Mercifully, Tim was also enrolled at Marist Brothers, so I had him and our small group of friends from primary school, who continued to weather the bullying storm that swirled around me. When we were together, I felt strong and had a sense of belonging; when I was alone, I felt much more vulnerable, and some of the worst taunting came from boys much bigger and older than I was, with whom I could never physically compete. They delighted in targeting the 'ballet boy', and rarely missed an opportunity to do so.

The walk to the bus stop was the most dangerous part of my day. Out of the view of parents and teachers, it was open slather for abuse. After my cap was thrown out of the bus window several times – which then necessitated getting off the bus to retrieve it – I learnt to sit in the front seats, near the driver. I also walked several stops ahead to catch the bus, which meant many of the bullies were on earlier buses and I had a more peaceful trip home. This did not stop them, however, from opening the windows and yelling 'Hey, poofter!' as they passed me on the bus.

Despite all of this, there were some places where I found acceptance and peace at my new school. I particularly loved being in the art room, where a fantastic art teacher, Mrs Lowe, nurtured my creative leanings. I was so happy there that I devised a scam in which I told my year level teacher that Mrs Lowe had asked me to go to the art room, and then once I had been excused, I went to the art room and would tell Mrs Lowe that the year level teacher had allowed me to go to the art room as I was so far ahead in the work we were doing. Flagrant lies all round, but my art really benefitted from it (at the sad expense of my maths).

Another great source of solace was the school's headmaster, Brother Justin. He was interested in my dancing and always very supportive, when so many others considered it an inappropriate choice for a young boy. Brother Justin was so encouraging that when the Scottish Ballet came to Perth, starring Margot Fonteyn, at the same time that I was performing as a child extra in *The Nutcracker* Act II, he announced in the school newsletter that 'year 5 student David McAllister will be partnering Margot Fonteyn at His Majesty's Theatre'. Something of an overreach – Fonteyn and I weren't even on stage at the same time – but very kind and quite amusing.

My parents had also given me a great gift: I was resilient. Wrapped in their love, and so utterly determined that ballet was where I belonged, I had the strength to block out the bullying as best I could and carry on. This was a pattern throughout my life – adversity made me more determined. *I'll show them*, I thought, *one day I will be famous, and that will be my revenge.*

Another chance to work towards my career aspirations, and maybe find the fame that I dreamt of, came when the London Festival Ballet visited Perth in 1975 with Rudolf Nureyev's *The Sleeping Beauty*. Once again, the call came from Perth City Ballet's artistic leader, Diana Waldron, who had been tasked with the job of finding four boys to perform as pages in this mammoth touring production. Each of us had to be no taller than 4 foot 6 (140 centimetres), a requirement I easily met. It was exciting to be part of a professional show again, and this one was to include the man who was possibly the biggest star in the ballet world as well as the catalyst for my desire to begin ballet. Our group arrived at the stage door of the Perth Entertainment Centre, and from the outset it seemed that all was not well. The company manager assigned to us looked concerned and there was a lot of chat about how short we were. It turned out that the paperwork had been incorrect, and the height requirement was meant to read 'no taller than 5 foot 6 (170 centimetres)' – a whole foot taller than any of us.

It was decided that we would put on the costumes and see what 'Rudi' thought. We looked rather swamped in the lavish and ill-fitting Nicholas Georgiadis–designed costumes. As we came down the sweeping staircase in the prologue scene, there was a very loud and adamant 'No!' yelled over the front-of-house microphone, after which we were quickly ushered off the stage. We had just been sacked by Rudolf Nureyev. As a consolation prize, we were all given tickets to see the opening night performance, which would now not include us. I was heartbroken and in such a state of self-pity that I sulked on my bed and refused to go to see the production. That lasted about an hour, after which I decided to swallow my pride and see the show.

A good thing, too, as it was one of those magical nights in the theatre that still looms large in my memory. The production was majestic and opulent in the extreme. It planted a seed that blossomed forty years later, inspiring me to take on *The Sleeping Beauty* as the first ballet I staged. I had never seen this style of show, with its huge headdresses, pannier skirts and sky-high wigs – it inspired me in my 'dress-up' styling at home. I had a skirt that my aunt had made me as a birthday present (it's a long story, but it was one of my absolute favourite presents ever). I dug it out of the play box and managed to attach a steel hoop fashioned from some bracing that had recently come on a pallet of bricks for one of Dad's home DIY projects. I then used packing string to mould the hoops into the pannier shape. I spent many hours parading around the back veranda in the style of the courtiers in *The Sleeping Beauty,* believing I was every bit as exotically decked out as the dancers of the Festival Ballet.

After picking myself up from this career misstep, I blundered on, regardless. I was cast in the role of Nancy in the school's production of *Oliver* – as an all-boys school, we had to have boys in some girls' roles. I was okay with this, even though I knew it would be further grist for the bullying mill. I was also the understudy in the lead role and, in a theme that recurred throughout my life, the classic theatre cliché happened: the boy originally cast as Oliver never turned up to rehearsals. To my delight, the director made us swap roles, and I performed as Oliver wearing a jaunty cap my mum usually teamed with her favourite pantsuit. Mum and Dad were surprised by my performance, as they hadn't thought of me as a singer. Though I'm not sure I was particularly talented, my voice had not yet broken so I could hit all the high notes. We had a record of the musical at home, so I studied the performance of the young boy playing Oliver closely, trying to copy him exactly.

Other school theatre endeavours were less successful. During one performance of *The Pirates of Penzance*, I had been asked to dance, and so I decided to do the tarantella from the Royal Academy of Dance syllabus, which I had been studying for my recent exam. As it turned out, my version of this rapid Italian folk dance was a pretty jarring moment in the evening. Another time, I let Brother Justin talk me into performing a liturgical dance during a Mass, which was another huge lowlight in my school social life. But as I say, I blundered on, regardless.

In senior school at the larger Churchlands campus, the bullying continued unabated. I managed to maintain a social group made up of misfits, including the unsporty (which at this time included boys who played soccer rather than Australian Rules), the super brainy (and super nerdy), and the downright socially unacceptable (including me, the one who did ballet). Phys. ed. was the worst lesson of the day: I had no hand-eye coordination, so I failed miserably at any kind of ball sport. Most of my time playing football was spent running away from the ball. I managed to swim quite well, and when the school built an Olympic-sized pool I achieved modest success. But generally, life moved slowly in those days; I endured school in the knowledge that a ballet class was never far away.

Later, in years 11 and 12, school life improved markedly with the arrival of girls, as the senior years were co-ed. Some of the girls I had known in primary school returned, and the boys' attention was suddenly diverted into showing off in front of them rather than worrying about what I was doing. All in all, it made school much more bearable.

In the ballet studio, things were much happier. I was growing stronger in my technique, doing well in exams, and working as hard as I could at every opportunity. I adored every minute of it and was determined that this would be my career. I wanted to go to The Australian Ballet School – I had dreamt of it ever since I watched The Australian Ballet perform *Cinderella* with my granny as a young child – and everything I did was with that goal in mind.

Then, one balmy autumn evening in 1978, when I was fourteen, something wonderful happened. Miss Hodgkinson called my parents in for a talk, and when they arrived, somewhat mystified, I was told to go and wait on the porch of the old Progress Hall. Thanks to my determined eavesdropping, I was able to hear most of the conversation. Miss Hodgkinson told my parents she thought it was time for me to audition for The Australian Ballet School, with Perth auditions scheduled for later in the year. I was beside myself with anticipation. The evening was closing in, and as I sat dreaming about moving to Melbourne and dancing full-time, I swear I saw a falling star. I took this as a sign and also an opportunity to make a wish: that I would be accepted into The Australian Ballet and have a career as a dancer.

My parents, who came home with the audition forms, were not convinced. They thought I was too young – and even though I was fourteen, I was a mere 155 centimetres tall, skinny, and had only just hit puberty. I still looked and sounded like a little boy. My parents had come to accept that ballet was probably going to be my career in some form – mostly because I had told them so incessantly since I was seven, but also because this claim had been supported by ballet teachers and exam results. By this stage I was also taking Sunday ballet classes with the West Australian Ballet.

The sticking point was that it would mean sending me, on my own, 3400 kilometres away to Melbourne. Had the school been in Perth, my parents might have been talked around. Still, my excitement was unstoppable, and I badgered and badgered with all the enthusiasm of a fourteen-year-old. Then I tried a new tactic: 'Perhaps I could just audition for practice,' I cajoled. 'I probably won't get in anyway.' Somehow this worked, and they agreed to let me audition. We filled out the forms and took the required photos of me posing in my ballet gear in the lounge room in the basic ballet positions: arms in *bras bas*, first position, second position, with the feet crossed over in fifth position and also a *dégagé* to the side. By this time, my sister, Di, was working in the mailroom at St John Ambulance, so Mum gave her the precious envelope with my audition forms and photos and asked her to mail it the next day.

As my mother entered the audition date into the family diary, we realised there was a problem: it was going to occur on the same weekend the entire family was planning a trip away. 'I'm not going,' I announced. 'I'm going to the ballet school audition.' I wasn't swayed, and so it was arranged that I would stay with my nan, who dutifully took me there in her white Mini. During the drive I had a slight panic about being late, because she had trouble finding the venue. We eventually arrived, just in time.

I walked up to the desk where Margaret Scott, the school's revered director – who much later I came to know as Maggie – was seated. In a studio behind her, Ray Powell, the company's ballet master (in other words, a teacher in a ballet company), was preparing to teach the class. 'Next,' Maggie said and I approached. 'David McAllister,' I said, and watched her eyes run down the list. 'I don't seem to have your name here,' she said, finally looking up. My heart sank. *Not there?* On the verge of tears, I turned silently and started to walk away. Then Maggie said: 'Oh no, it's all right, come here. What's your name?' She added my name to the bottom of her list, and then told me, to my unending relief and delight, to go and get changed, and warm up for class.

I went into a tiny room and changed into my ballet clothes, which by that time consisted of black tights (and a homemade 'support' or 'jockstrap', as they didn't stock them in the ballet shop we went to), white socks with black shoes, and the obligatory white T-shirt.

There I met two other boys auditioning, both of whom seemed enormous. Together we went into the class, instructed by Ray, and he asked us to do a string of steps I'd never done before, including a double *tour en l'air*.

'What's that?' I asked.

'Oh, well you *relevé* in fifth, you jump and turn twice, then land back in fifth,' he explained, describing the process step by step that began with rising up on the balls of the feet in the classic ballet position, the legs positioned one in front of the other.

Okay, I'll give it a go, I thought to myself. I watched the other two do it and thought I'd have no trouble. When I tried, I wasn't terrible, but not perfect, either. I was willing to try anything, though, if they would just let me into their school.

At the end of the class, Maggie thanked all the dancers for coming and called me over to get some more details, given that I had effectively walked in off the street. She then looked up at me and said: 'Would you be interested in coming to The Australian Ballet School?' to which I immediately replied, 'Oh yes, Miss Scott.' She nodded and said, 'Well, will you tell your parents that we're very interested? Perhaps it would be best if I gave them a call.'

'Great!' I enthused and walked out on cloud nine. All my dreams were starting to come true.

The audition was on Sunday, and that night, the rest of my family returned from the weekend away to be greeted with my enthusiasm about my audition success. The next day, Maggie rang and spoke with my mum. I was listening. I heard my mum say: 'Oh no, I don't think we want to send David to Melbourne, but I'll have to speak with my husband.' Once Dad got home, the dramas began. They were both astonished that I'd been accepted, and now they were faced with a difficult decision, not made any easier by my theatrics in the background.

Maggie had done her best to talk them around. A big concern for my parents – apart from sending a teenager, who looked like a little kid, to the other side of the country on his own – was my schooling.

'How will he finish his education?' my mother asked. 'He's only in year 10.'

'Well, we offer correspondence education,' Maggie told her.

This exchange triggered a very long conversation between my parents. Finally, they came to a decision, and it was the one I didn't want to hear: no, I was too young. It felt like my whole world was crashing down around me, and in my typical style I turned on my heel and stormed down the hallway to my bedroom, shouting 'You've ruined my life!' as I went. I threw myself on my bed and devoted quite some time to Definitely Not Talking to my parents.

Eventually, I calmed down. Mum, in her usual way, tried to smooth things over. 'It will be for the best,' she said. 'This way you can keep studying, and if they want you badly enough you can go when you finish school.'

'But I'll be too old by then,' I complained, although I was wrong about that.

My dad was, of course, on a unity ticket with her. 'Your education is important, David,' he said. 'And what if you get injured, or you're not good enough to make a career in ballet?'

These were all perfectly reasonable questions. After all, Martin Rubinstein, a former star of the Borovansky Ballet who had examined me a couple of times in my Royal Academy of Dance exams, and with whom I had taken some classes at a summer school before my audition, had said to Miss Hodgkinson: 'He's short, he's going to have a very limited career, but he's good enough to do it. It's not going to be easy, but if he's to give it a shot he has to go to Melbourne.' His comments had been relayed back to my parents, in whom it had sown enough doubt to make them insist that I finish school first. In hindsight, my parents' decision was the right one, not only because of my schooling but also my maturity. I needed a little more time.

I was left to nurse my disappointment and work through my end of a bargain I reached with my parents: I must not just show up at school but pass my HSC. Then, if they still wanted me, I could go to The Australian Ballet School. Once I had come to terms with this, I then broached the subject of my missing audition application with my sister. 'You know, they didn't have my name on the list,' I said to her. 'Well,' she replied, 'I didn't send your application. I didn't want you to go, so I didn't send it.' I couldn't believe that she had tried to sabotage my big chance and made the usual fuss to her and my parents, but deep down I couldn't help but feel a bit chuffed that my sister loved me that much.

Once I regrouped, I became all the more determined to get to The Australian Ballet School. The following year, when I was in year 11, we planned a family holiday 'over east' to Melbourne, and I saw this as the perfect opportunity to visit the school while I was there. It was a nightmare trip, with all seven of us squeezed into the Holden Premier – four in the back and three in the front – on the seemingly endless road to the other side of the country.

I hadn't been allowed to audition that year as my parents were adamant that I had to complete year 12, so Maggie Scott had rung my parents to ask where I was.

'Well, he's not going until next year, if he goes at all,' my mum replied firmly.

'Yes,' said Maggie, 'but I still wanted to see him.'

Once we made it to Melbourne and had done a few days of sightseeing, I decided that a Friday afternoon might be the ideal time to ask my family to trek across an unfamiliar city in peak-hour traffic to a suburb called Flemington to visit the ballet school. The drive was a complete disaster, full of one-way streets and trams and more traffic than we'd ever seen. Finally, we made it to the elusive suburb, and Dad pulled up close enough for me to read the sign out the front: The Australian Ballet School. 'Okay, that's fine,' I chimed from the back seat. 'We can go now.' Dad looked at me in the rear-view mirror: 'You are joking. We have just driven for an hour and a half to find it, and you're not even going to go inside?'

In my mind, I was worrying about what to say if people asked me why I was there. 'No, I just wanted to see it,' I said.

'You get inside,' my dad said, and I knew my dad well enough to take my seatbelt off and do exactly that. I gingerly opened the door and stuck my head in. Inside was a particularly ugly foyer with a couple of settees and a wooden desk, where the receptionist usually sat, except she had gone home. Mercifully, being a Friday afternoon, no one else was there and the company was away. I remember seeing an honour board and placed next to it was a very glamorous photograph of a woman – the only glamorous thing in the foyer. I was to find out much later that it was a photograph of The Australian Ballet's founding artistic director, Dame Peggy van Praagh, which is still in the Ballet Centre today.

'Okay, we can go now,' I said when I returned to the car, and thankfully this time Dad didn't argue. I'd seen enough to know it was where I belonged.

Halfway through my year 12, we received the audition papers for The Australian Ballet School and this time I could fill them out happily, taking the required photos and then running the film to the chemist to be developed. We took some photos in front of the pool – god knows why – and then on the front veranda, where I tried a little too hard to be arty; all they really wanted to see was whether I had grown and was reasonably in proportion. By this time I had indeed grown a bit and was taking five dance classes a week. But my repertoire was still limited, and I hadn't done any partnering work at all. All of a sudden, the stakes felt very high.

I was instructed to present myself one evening at His Majesty's Theatre for the audition. When I got there and registered I went to the change room to find that this time there were three other boys there for the audition, all of whom seemed big and muscular to me. *Oh my god*, I thought as I changed.

It was, by any measure, a remarkably talented group of boys. Among them was Steven Heathcote – later to become a principal dancer with The Australian Ballet, and whom we all called Steve – and Paul Mercurio, who would be a star of Sydney Dance Company before electrifying the big screen as the lead in Baz Luhrmann's *Strictly Ballroom*. Also there was Darren Spowart, who would later join the company and become one of my best mates. The boys seemed to know each other, while I didn't know anyone, not even any of the girls who were there to audition.

Robert Ray, one of the teachers from The Australian Ballet School, was giving the class in the studios of the West Australian Ballet. Before class began, we each had to stand in front of Maggie and Robert – I guess there were about forty kids auditioning in total – and do a *dégagé* right then left, bend forward, and bend backwards. I'd done this before and had been expecting it, so I concentrated on trying to be as flexible as possible. Then we did barre, which is how each ballet class begins, with exercises carried out with one hand holding the barre to help with balance. We then had to do the splits – I was buoyed by this as I was actually able to do them, a reasonably rare achievement for a boy.

I wondered how I compared with the other boys. Paul seemed very grown-up and strong to me, and also incredibly cool – he rode a motorbike. Steve also seemed mature – he was tall, muscular and handsome. Darren and I were skinnier and smaller, and I remember panicking slightly that they all seemed so talented. By the end of the class – remembering what had happened the first time I auditioned – my heart was beating hard.

Maggie called all four boys into the corridor, while the girls remained in the classroom. 'Oh, it's very nice to see so many boys,' she said, and added: 'and I'd really like to offer all of you places at The Australian Ballet School for next year.' We all cheered, and I thought, *Thank god, we're all in.*

Back in the change room, Paul congratulated everyone and organised for us all to swap phone numbers so we could get together before school started in the new year. And we did exactly that – right before we were all set to travel to Melbourne, he organised a party, which was actually held at Steve's home, and we were all invited. Paul was friendly and outgoing, Steve and Darren a little more reserved. But they were now my friends, my classmates, my future competitors. And this time, true to their word and with my HSC successfully completed, my parents made arrangements for me to take up the offer and make the long journey across to Melbourne.

I was delirious with happiness. I was leaving school behind and finally going where I knew I wanted, needed, to be. I would be in a world of people just like me.

I was going to be free.

CHAPTER 3

Dance school daze

I didn't care that The Australian Ballet School dance uniform was hideous. And it truly was. It wasn't jiffies territory, but it wasn't far off: we wore a black singlet with white stitching, grey tights, white socks to the knee and black ballet shoes. And even though this uniform was indisputably ugly, it didn't faze me because it was all part of my aspiration to dance, which was slowly coming true. I am not sure if it was because I was scarred by the jiffies I had had to wear all those years ago, or if, after years of being an outsider at school, I just wanted to make sure that I fitted in perfectly as I started my time at the ballet school, but I was pathologically focused on ensuring I had exactly what the school's information pack had asked for, with no deviations.

The trouble for us lads from Western Australia was that we had to arrive in Melbourne ready for the first day of school, and in Perth in 1980, the availability of such things as dance accoutrements was extremely limited. My mum found some black singlets without the white stitching, but I rejected those immediately as not being *exactly right*. Getting the correct make-up was even harder. We needed to find the extremely traditional, professional Leichner-brand greasepaint sticks in ivory, carmine, brick red, lake and black. The school also suggested we buy a fishing tackle box to store our make-up. In Melbourne, you could simply take yourself to a ballet shop and buy all of these things, but in Perth, we had no idea where to even find them. There was a lot of running around done by my ever-patient parents – and the items that we couldn't locate we had to wait to buy as soon as we arrived in Melbourne. Ironically, I don't think we ever used the rainbow sticks we searched so hard to find: by the time we needed stage make-up, the greasepaints had been replaced by the trusty Max Factor Pan Stik number 2.

While all of this flapping was going on – mostly by me – my parents pondered the far knottier problem of where I was going to live in Melbourne. Luckily, Mum and Dad had a friend from church called Irene Hanneberry, who was originally from Melbourne. After her husband passed away, Irene moved back to her home town with three of her daughters, Genevieve, Mary and Anne, while her son, Michael, went to work in the north of Western Australia. When they lived in Perth, the Hanneberrys had taken in a young guy from Melbourne to board with them, so Mum contacted Irene and asked if she'd be interested in doing something similar in Melbourne. Given Irene had a spare room, she immediately agreed, to my parents' immense relief.

The arrangement was that we paid Irene $20 a week – $10 for board, and $10 for food. On top of that, there were ballet school fees to pay, although they were not particularly onerous: $450 a year, which was paid in three instalments at the start of each term. Because I was living away from home and Dad was the sole income earner, I qualified for the Tertiary Education Assistance Scheme (TEAS), which had been introduced by the Whitlam government in 1973 to encourage more students to undertake higher education. That covered my board but, even better, it allowed for three return trips home to Perth annually, which meant I could fly home for each of the school holidays.

In January 1981, I said goodbye to my brothers and sister in Perth and headed to Melbourne with Mum and Dad for my great adventure. It was my first flight on a plane, which I was extremely excited about. It had been a tradition for the whole family to go to the airport whenever anyone was leaving or arriving, but this was the first time it was me disappearing through the glass doors. We flew on the Ansett 'midnight horror', which left around midnight and arrived in Melbourne at 6 am. As we were staying for the first few days in a motel, we had to walk around all morning with our luggage before we could check in. It was both exciting and daunting to walk around the huge city as it woke up, discovering my new home. As soon as we finally got settled, we bought all the extra things I needed for school. A few days later, it was time to head to my new home in Bloom Street, Moonee Ponds.

The Hanneberrys' house was perfect – not only was it close to the tramline and the Ballet Centre, but I had my own room for the first time in my life. It had a window that looked out to a walkway along the side of the house edged with lovely greenery. The interior design was 70s cool, featuring a bold brown geometric wallpaper with green and brown Marimekko-style print curtains. I absolutely loved it. I hung a ballet poster on the wall and felt at home straightaway. Irene and the girls generously absorbed me into their family – Irene made dinner for us all every night and packed me a lunch for school every day, and the girls were always friendly and kind. My parents called most Sundays after 6 pm, when STD (long-distance) telephone rates were cheaper. I went to church every Sunday at St Monica's just down the street for the whole of my first year at school – more out of habit and not wanting to disappoint my devout mum than anything. In some way it was also a connection to my life at home, but over time, the habit fell by the wayside as my devotion to ballet took over.

At last, after what seemed like an eternity, my first day at The Australian Ballet School was here. In my excitement, I arrived at the Flemington studios ridiculously early and then was too nervous to go in, so I sat out the front on a pine-log seat, quietly fretting until some of the other boys got there. Steve Heathcote and Paul Mercurio appeared at the designated time with a group of other kids and, almost weak with relief to see some familiar faces, I followed them in.

There were eighteen first-year boys, and we were all in one class. The Ballet Centre housed the company and the school, which shared its four studios. The largest studio, studio 1, was the company's, as was the smallest, studio 4. Studios 2 and 3 were used by the school, although when the company was touring we occasionally used all the studios. We often passed the company's dancers in the hallways, but there was no fraternisation between us – we were very much the students and in awe of the professional dancers; they in turn had little time for the students in the school. We knew who they all were and aspired to be just like them.

After a brief orientation, we were welcomed by Margaret Scott, not only the school's director but in many ways its heart and soul. Maggie was born in 1922 in Johannesburg, where she grew up with older twin sisters, Joan and Barbara, and learnt ballet from a prominent local teacher. Her talent took her to England, where she joined the famous Sadler's Wells company and then the Ballet Rambert. She toured to Australia with the company in the late 1940s, but a serious back injury meant she stayed behind in Melbourne for treatment. There she met a medical researcher, Derek Denton, whom she later married in England before returning with him to his adopted home town of Melbourne. She began a teaching career in Melbourne and was one of the driving forces in establishing a national ballet company in 1962 under the direction of Peggy van Praagh. Two years later, she became the founding director of The Australian Ballet School.

Maggie was formidable and straight-talking, but also kind and practical. She was fiercely intelligent and had no time for drama queens or whingers. Everyone was at least a little scared of her, and desperate to impress her. Always rail thin and balletic, she wore her long hair swept up at the sides and in a low bun, usually with some kind of adornment on top. When she was teaching, she wore pink T-bar teaching shoes and blue checked pants with a short-sleeved knitted top. Away from the classroom, she was usually in classic skirts and tops, and always immaculately groomed. While she was considerate, she was never effusive – I didn't have any real sense of what Maggie thought of me or my talent at the time, but looking back, I can see she was extremely supportive and encouraging.

Though I had met her at my auditions, where she played a key role in my journey to The Australian Ballet School, Maggie was now a pivotal figure in determining my future, so on that first day I hung on every word as she gave us an introductory talk. One of the things she stressed was that no one was to smoke in the building: 'I've seen a tutu go up in a flash!' she said in her no-nonsense way. 'And up in the roof, there's all these tutus, so you just can't smoke!' And then she turned very serious indeed. 'You are here to work,' she instructed.

'I don't care what's happening in your private life – you leave that at the door. When you walk into the Ballet Centre, it's all about the training.'

With that somewhat sobering talk out of the way, we were sent into our first class with our main teacher, Paul Hammond. I walked in and saw a sea of unfamiliar faces – the only boys I recognised were Steve and Paul. Darren Spowart hadn't arrived yet as he was working and had to give notice, so he was to start two weeks after the rest of us. I wondered, somewhat anxiously, how good the other boys were and if I would be able to keep up.

My nervousness wasn't helped by the sight of a boy called Alan Simmons, who was warming up on one side of the room. I didn't even know that warming up was what you were supposed to do before a class – I was just sitting there waiting for something to happen. Alan was doing the splits up the wall with his legs threaded up behind the barre. A slight panic clutched my chest. *Oh my god, there's no way I can do that*, I thought. *I'm going to be the worst person in this class.* But then the class started. Paul Hammond was lovely and very quietly spoken, and his class was not as difficult as I feared. Slowly, I started to relax.

I remained a little worried about my size. While I wasn't the smallest guy in the class – I was probably about average – I was still pretty underdeveloped and weak, and once we started pas de deux work, at which I was truly terrible, I knew I needed to build myself up. At seventeen, I was very much in the throes of puberty, with terrible acne galloping up both cheeks and little tufts of wispy facial hair where I would have liked some manly stubble to be. While I had grown and filled out a bit, I needed more strength if I was to cope with the physical demands of a career in ballet, so I did push-ups every night at home in an effort to grow stronger. The school also sent us to the Debney Park Community Centre nearby, where we were made to run around the oval and play basketball, which I was hopeless at given my complete lack of hand-eye coordination. One day, cranky at what seemed to me the ludicrousness of the training they were asking us to do at Debney Park, I decided that instead of running around the oval, I would do *jeté élancé* (a turning *grand jeté*, which is basically doing the splits in the air as you jump, then swivelling fully on the ground before launching yourself forward into the next *jeté*), to the great amusement of my classmates. I couldn't sustain it for very long and I stopped about two-thirds of the way around the oval, exhausted, while the others watched and laughed. I felt I had made my point.

After the first two weeks, when I had yet to make any close friends, Darren Spowart arrived. I wasn't particularly looking forward to seeing him – at the auditions in Perth, he had been the one I had warmed to least of the three other boys. He had struck me as aloof, but also a bit of a smart-arse: the guy with the one-liners, the answers for every question. He seemed to be the opposite of my wide-eyed enthusiasm and naivety, and I had already decided that I wasn't going to like him.

During his first week at the school, Darren was lying on a couch in the green room (the rather dingy common room where all the students and company dancers hung out in between classes and rehearsals) when Paul Mercurio – still, in my eyes, incredibly cool and grown-up – walked past him and said: 'Get up, Darren, you don't own the place.' Darren looked a little taken aback, so I went over and started talking to him, and something just clicked – from that moment we became firm friends. One of the reasons we became so close was that Darren was also homestaying at a place two tram stops from mine, so we'd jump on the tram together after school and see each other again in the mornings. Once I got to know him, I realised it was his worldliness that had initially frightened me, but it sat alongside a great sense of humour and the same 'bun-head' obsession with ballet that I had. I enjoyed getting around this big new city with someone who, although younger, was much more grown-up and at home in the world than I was.

Darren and I started going to parties together. As I had never been popular at school, I hadn't been invited to many parties, but now there were parties to attend all the time and I was grateful to have someone to go with. Often they were fancy dress, so Darren and I would raid an op shop for a costume or buy something we could adapt, and we became a bit of a unit. Darren found a job washing dishes at a restaurant close to his home, so on Saturdays we'd go to class in the morning, then I'd usually go home, complete my homework and perhaps have a nanna nap while Darren went to work until about 10 pm. I'd set my alarm to head out and meet him after work, and then we'd go to a party together. I'd usually stay until about midnight before heading home, making sure I caught the last tram. Suffice to say, I was never a wild child.

I was such a good boy, in fact, that I hadn't touched a drop of alcohol before I turned eighteen. Hard to believe, I know, but given my mild social activities, I was never going to be a big boozer. When I turned eighteen at the end of my first year at ballet school, Darren threw a party for me, where we drank a liqueur called Drops on the Rocks that we mixed with lemonade. Although I honestly thought it was disgusting, I was thrilled to be doing adult things.

The Australian Ballet School's lively social scene was what you would expect given it was made up of a group of energetic young people, many of whom were living away from home for the first time. The drinks of choice at these weekend parties were Southern Comfort and Coke or very cheap wine. At Darren's eighteenth, which was about six months after mine, I tried my first Southern and Coke, and shortly after that got completely hammered for the first time, to the point where I threw up. You can understand that this is no longer on my list of preferred beverages!

While Darren and I became very close, there was never anything sexual between us. We never talked about it, and to be honest I'm not sure we even thought about it. I was still very unsure about my sexuality, but I'd pushed that to one side to make way for my complete fixation on ballet. This way of thinking led the two of us to some pretty wholesome nights in. We used to go to Darren's place because he had his own room *and* a cassette player, which we felt was the height of luxury living. We'd sit there and listen to Act II of *Giselle* together, and later we bought a recording of *Scheherazade* and did the same thing.

At the ballet school, we continued to be challenged. While Paul Hammond and to a lesser extent Maggie were our main classical ballet teachers, we also had the occasional guest teacher such as Lucette Aldous (who taught the first-year girls and whom I still idolised, having seen her dance with Nureyev in *Don Quixote* all those years ago), Marika Besobrasova and a wonderful eccentric Russian called Janina Cunova, who was actually the second-year girls' teacher (our classes were strictly gender segregated except for pas de deux). Janina used to set an exercise and then turn her back on us as she applied lipstick in the mirror, so we foolishly assumed she wasn't watching us. At the end of the exercise, she would turn around and give five minutes of corrections, as she had been watching in the mirror to see who was working hard even without the teacher's gaze shining on them. And she was merciless: 'You know, when I go to New York, the people take my classes, they think I'm wonderful teacher. When I come here, you ignore me.' And then she'd ask sternly: 'Why you want to be dancer if you stand like that? You stand like that, I don't see dancer, you know.' I loved doing her classes and learnt a great deal from her. I also developed a pretty good impersonation of her unique accent, which I still pull out to entertain at dinner parties.

Aside from classical ballet, we also had contemporary classes with Jenny Kinder, who left midway through the year to found Tasdance in Launceston, then with Eric Sennen who had danced in Europe, from whom we learnt a variation of the Graham technique, the modern dance technique that was created by the famous American contemporary dance trailblazer Martha Graham. In second year we switched to the Cunningham technique, another contemporary technique closer to ballet but which incorporated many of the choreographic idiosyncrasies of its founder, Merce Cunningham. Robert Ray gave these classes, and it was good to train with him after having enjoyed the audition class he taught us in Perth. We also learnt character with Christine Howard, which I loved. The character classes entailed learning the folkloric dance technique, which included a variety of East European dances such as mazurkas and czardas. Christine had been a dancer in the Melbourne-based Kolobok Dance Company and had taken on the character training from Madam Berezowsky, who founded the Kolobok company. I took to these classes very naturally, with all the deep knee bends and jumps – finally, my muscular thighs came into their own! When she was our guest teacher, Lucette warned us against developing big, muscular thighs, and showed us how to massage our legs in a way that would streamline the muscles. I always had a bit of a love-hate relationship with my legs, and Lucette's advice only made me doubt their aesthetic more.

There were theory classes, too, including Benesh notation with Barbara Nimmo. Benesh notation is a way of writing dance movements on a musical stave developed by British mathematician Rudolf Benesh and his wife, Joan. While other people have developed various ways of notating dance movements, Benesh is an extremely adaptable system that can be used to notate any human movement. Made up of various dots, dashes and lines, it was interesting but always a bit of a puzzle to me. Barbara was wonderful, though, and brought it to life in a way that made sense to a very unmathematical ballet student like me. She also provided great pastoral care to us young boys, although she was only a couple of years older than we were. Dance history, with Edward Pask, came much more naturally to me, as did music appreciation with one of the class pianists, Jerri Mann. On top of this, in one of the school terms we were bussed to the National Gallery of Victoria once a week for art appreciation, where some of the cooler kids would wag the tutorials and instead go for cappuccinos at the Two Way cafe on Elizabeth Street, while the goody-two-shoes like me would stay and absorb the lectures from the curators.

Just when we had settled into a routine with our first-year classes, Maggie lobbed a grenade into the room. There were only six boys in second year and eighteen boys in first year – a fact that had generated a few whispers about the talent to be found in the first-year ranks. At the end of class one day, Maggie came in and announced they were splitting our first-year class to even out the numbers between first and second year. This meant eleven boys were staying in first year and seven boys were to train with the second years. None of us knew who would be in which group, so when a note went up on the noticeboard the next day, we all raced to see which group we were in. I was listed in group B with six other boys, and immediately felt disappointed, not realising that it was the B group that would be dancing with the second years. My friends were all there: Steve, Paul, Darren and another good friend of mine, Darryl Sim.

Our teacher for the 'first-year boys B' class that was combined with the second years was Bruce Morrow, and I adored him. He was about my height, perhaps even shorter, and he loved setting intricate pirouette exercises, which we called 'turning'. As I loved turning, I relished the chance to push myself at something for which I had a natural aptitude. Pas de deux classes were another matter. I'd already struggled in first year with pas de deux because I wasn't strong enough to be a reliable partner to the girls, and once we'd been bumped up into second year, my weakness became even more pronounced.

The second-year girls were glad to have more boys joining the class – otherwise they had to miss out or double up on partners – but I think the ones paired with the first-year boys definitely felt they had drawn the short straw. Ideally in pas de deux, the girl should be about a head shorter than the boy – that way, when she's *en pointe* she's about the same height or just shorter than the boy. The first girl I was paired with was a good height for me, but she wasn't the smallest girl in the class, and I was far from the strongest boy. The teachers seemed to have paired those of us who were weak at pas de deux – Darren also struggled with it – with girls who would strengthen us and force us to work harder, while the tiniest girls were paired with the strong boys.

It was really tough, and I worried about my partnering ceaselessly. I couldn't promenade – a staple of pas de deux work that requires the boy to hold the girl lightly by the waist and walk in a circle with her staying *en pointe*. If you don't do it properly you can easily make the girl lose her balance, which in my case meant both of us constantly stumbling over. Eventually, though, after many push-ups and some embarrassments, I improved. I can clearly remember the first time I managed an overhead lift without either of us falling over – it felt like I had won the lottery. I think it took the entire year for me to master this lift – I might even have been in my second year before I managed it.

Otherwise, things were going well at the school. One day in first year, Maggie called me to her office and, terrified, I wondered what I had done. To my great surprise and delight, she told me I had been awarded The Australian Ballet Society scholarship, one of a clutch of scholarships that were available to students, which everyone seemed to know about except me. It was worth $500, which effectively wiped out my fees for the year and gave me some great news to share with my parents when they rang the following Sunday night. I was lucky enough to win the scholarship again in my second year, which was a huge benefit to my family, taking care of my fees once again. I felt as though I was helping out, as I understood that my study was a big commitment for the family, with two other brothers still at school and all the expenses that came with me living in Melbourne. It was unusual for a student to win the scholarship two years in a row, and looking back, I can see it was indicative of Maggie's great belief in me, given in her extremely 'hands-off' but quietly supportive way to avoid the appearance of favouring any dancer over another. She would never say, 'Oh, aren't you lovely?' but rather 'Ah! Point those feet!' I always felt, nonetheless, that she was watching out for all of us.

For the most part, we as students were all in it together – there weren't any 'stars' as there so often are in ballet schools. Having said that, some of us were given more opportunities to extend ourselves, firstly through being elevated into second year, and then in performance work. For example, Christine Howard put together a group called Smart Guys to perform a character dance, and I was chosen for this group, along with Darren and fellow 'first-year B' classmates Mark Kay and Darryl Sim. This ruffled a few feathers among some of the older boys, who felt that the first years were being given opportunities at their expense. Another time, an ABC TV program called *Beyond 2000* came to the school to shoot a show about Benesh notation. I was chosen along with a second-year student who was in my pas de deux class to learn a small segment of a *Swan Lake* pas de deux from the notation, which was then aired on television, to our huge excitement.

Generally, I had the feeling I was doing well. I loved every minute of being at the school – I could happily have stayed there all day and night. I was delighted to be living in Melbourne, and my host family, the Hanneberrys, were taking excellent care of me. Still, I was often homesick. Mum wrote me a letter every week and I wrote her one in return, and there were the regular Sunday night phone calls. Every now and then word swept through the school of a payphone that was jammed, allowing calls to anywhere in Australia for 10 cents, so we'd all rush to it to call our families. There was one at Flinders Street Station that was frequently jammed, and I remember going down there a couple of times to call home simply to hear my parents' voices.

A favourite activity for Darren and me was to go watch tapings of Bert Newton's show *New Faces* at the GTV9 studios. When they shot audience pans we'd wave frantically at the camera, and afterwards we'd ring home and say, 'Watch *New Faces*! We're on this week!' Yes, I was a little homesick, but returning to Perth every holiday kept it from becoming unbearable.

Darren and I continued our complete devotion to our studies but also took great delight in fostering new creative talents in other areas of our lives. Leading up to the first term break, we decided to make Easter eggs to take home with us and give to our families – god knows how we thought the chocolates were even going to survive the trip. We bought moulds and compound chocolate and it all turned into a disgusting mess, so was abandoned. We were also very interested in fashion, which, being the early 80s, was loud, attention-seeking and usually involved legwarmers. Just our thing! Everyone was into Staggers jeans, so we'd buy cheaper knock-off versions at Victoria Market and team them with a pair of legwarmers over the top. I desperately wanted to bleach my hair – which was very much in vogue at the time – but thought the ballet school might frown on it, so I resisted this urge.

The day before we were to fly home for that particular holiday, we realised we didn't have legwarmers to wear – I can't remember why we didn't think the ones we wore at school would suffice – and so we decided to knit a pair in a day to wear home. I was a pretty good knitter, a skill Mum had taught me, but I wasn't fast enough to knit a full-length pair of legwarmers in one day, so I cast off when they were only big enough to sit around my ankles. This meant I had what was effectively a knitted cuff around my jeans. Darren, more sensibly, had a jumper his mum had knitted for him that he cut the sleeves off and converted into two more meaningful legwarmers. We were still very much adolescents, wanting to return home and be seen as cool and grown-up, when we were really just daggy kids.

In October 1981, as my first year was drawing to a close, my ballet dream felt like it might come crashing down. When the company was performing in Melbourne, we all tried to attend as many shows as we could. We'd take the two trams down to the Palais Theatre in St Kilda, arriving right before the curtain went up, and if there were any spare seats we'd be able to take them. They were usually high up in the dress circle, but we didn't care; we were just thrilled to be there. Some nights we'd turn up and be crushed to find there were no spare seats, so to save disappointment we often went to dress rehearsals instead, which we were always allowed to watch. This particular time the company was performing *The Hunchback of Notre Dame*, and I'd been to both the dress rehearsal and opening night.

One night a week after the season opened, the unthinkable happened. Before the show, the dancers held the curtain, waiting to be presented with their contracts for the 1982 season. The contracts arrived, but they included the feared clauses that effectively demoted all of the principal dancers to soloists, which the dancers had been fighting for some time. As one, all the dancers sensationally went on strike and performances were cancelled in Melbourne and Sydney. The media were all over it, and we absorbed as much of it as we could. At the Ballet Centre, rumours were flying, and there was a strange, tense atmosphere in the building with the company dancers gone and the administrators with a crisis on their hands. About a week into the strike, which ultimately lasted for twenty-six days, the students gathered in the green room to be addressed by Kelvin Coe – who had become a spokesperson for the striking dancers – and some of the other company members. The dancers asked for our support, with the grim warning that if we didn't band together, it could be the end of The Australian Ballet.

I walked out of the meeting completely devastated. *I've just gotten here*, I thought, *and now there's not going to be a ballet company*. I had no idea what else I could do with my life – all I wanted, all I had ever wanted, was to be a dancer with The Australian Ballet. Eventually the strike ended, but even after the dancers had returned to work, the atmosphere remained extremely tense.

Part of the fallout from the strike was that many of the company's top dancers, including Kelvin, resigned, decimating its senior ranks. This meant that a lot of junior dancers were promoted and, in turn, most of the third-year students were suddenly absorbed into the company; even some of the most talented second-year dancers like Glen Harris (with whom I had been in some classes at the school) were rapidly given corps de ballet jobs. By the start of 1982, the company was so hungry for talent that it employed beyond the school, taking in talented dancers such as Josephine Smulders and Greg Horsman from the Victorian College of the Arts. The company's artistic director, Marilyn Jones, had resigned and was replaced by a caretaker director, Marilyn Rowe, a former ballerina who was respected by all – this was the 'breakthrough' move that convinced the dancers to return to work. Marilyn gave the company stability to continue but made clear that she would oversee the company only until a new artistic director was found. She managed to artistically lead the company for the rest of 1981 and all of the following year while also performing starring roles in a range of the repertoire. It was a herculean feat and she was a strong leader, but the company remained a fractious place with a high turnover of dancers. It was a very strange time to be around the Ballet Centre, and everything felt uncertain.

In the midst of this ongoing storm, opportunities trickled down to us in the school. As second years, we were doing the second-year curriculum with our former classmates from first year, so the group was re-amalgamated. However, because so many third years were taken into the company and the shortage of boys continued, we ended up doing a lot of work with the third years. Towards the end of the year, some of us, including Steve Heathcote and me, were chosen to go on a regional tour with The Dancers Company. This company was established in 1980 as a regional touring arm of The Australian Ballet. It is made up of graduating dancers from The Australian Ballet School who mainly perform the corps de ballet roles (ensemble dances) and dancers from the company who dance the leading roles. It was the highlight of the year for the third-year students and an opportunity to gain professional experience on stage, which included (most notably) being paid to perform. It was not common for second years to be selected for the tour, so I was excited when Dame Peggy chose me to dance the Peasant pas de deux in her production of *Giselle*. This pas de deux is often performed by quite senior dancers and is a joyous and bravura segment in the first act. Its relevance in the ballet is to provide a counterpoint to the more dramatic and ultimately tragic storyline of Giselle and her duplicitous lover, Albrecht, who dresses as a peasant to woo her while disguising his noble birth. For this tour, I was first cast and Steve was second cast, while a third-year boy was the cover. In ballet, these 'casting' decisions are usually made based on hierarchy, so the more senior people will be higher up the casting. To have two second years as numbers one and two on the list and a third year as a cover was very provocative.

I remember hearing later that the third-year boy in question had complained that we weren't even in third year and yet we had leading roles. Shortly after, we witnessed Dame Peggy call this boy over to her in the corridor. 'I hear you're not happy about the casting,' she said to him. 'The thing is that those two boys fit the costumes, and in a touring company, if you fit the costume, then you're cast. And I don't think you'll fit the costume, so you're learning it but you probably won't go on.' I am sure he didn't; it was an early lesson in the harshness of life on the stage.

On tour, I did most of the shows featuring the Peasant pas de deux with Kathy Downey (a talented and petite third-year girl), sharing the role with Steve, who also danced in the other performances. Finally, we arrived in Perth, where I was desperate to give a big hometown performance in front of my family and friends. But it wasn't to be. During the dress rehearsal, I was trying to perfect a double *tour en l'air* to one knee, which I hadn't been doing well, when I landed awkwardly and sprained my ankle. It wasn't a bad sprain, but a sprain nonetheless, so instead of wowing my home town, I was confined to rest, ice and elevation. I was lucky that it healed quickly, because while I missed the entire Perth season, I was able to dance during the Geraldton leg of the tour, and my family drove up to see me perform, which was marvellous.

Later in the year, we had the annual graduation performance. One of the ballets we did that year was Sir Frederick Ashton's *Les Patineurs*. In it, I danced the Blue Boy with two third-year girls, while Steve danced the White Couple pas de deux with Ulrike Lytton, another third-year student. Once again we had landed what were basically the two lead roles, while other third years were in the corps de ballet. By this stage it was pretty clear that my career – and

Steve's for that matter – was going well. Maggie had brought in Dame Peggy to coach us for *Les Patineurs*, and Kelvin also helped us with some of the Blue Boy dance, and my awe of him continued. I remember Maggie, never one to overdo the compliments, coming backstage after the show and saying, in her terribly cultured voice, 'Bravo, darling, bravooooooo'. At that moment, we knew that we had triumphed. I was also exhilarated to learn that Kelvin was in the audience for the performance.

As 1982 came to a close, following the performance of our final show of *Les Patineurs*, Maggie came into our dressing room and said: 'Steven and David, I need to see you tomorrow morning at 9 am in my office.' *Oh shit*, I thought, *what on earth is this about?* My sister, Di, had come over from Perth to see the show and so I fretted alongside her, wondering what Maggie was going to say. I arrived at Maggie's office dutifully at 9 am the next day where, along with Marilyn Rowe, she was meeting with the third-year students to tell them if they were going to have a job in the company. The third years, waiting anxiously to go in, looked at Steve and me sideways with that *What the hell are you doing here?* look. Many of them came out with ashen faces, as not many from that year were given contracts; in fact, only one boy, Brent Iwanoczko, was given a contract, as were a couple of girls.

At last it was my turn to go in. Maggie told me that Steve and I were to be seconded into the company for three months: we were to do the *Spartacus* season, that was all, and then return to the school to do our third year. I had been entertaining a faint hope that we were about to be given jobs, and this was the next best thing – I was thrilled. At the beginning of our third year in 1983, Steve and I launched straight into classes with the company to learn *Spartacus*. A couple of days later, the newly appointed artistic director of The Australian Ballet arrived. Her name was Maina Gielgud, a former dancer with companies across Europe and an internationally renowned guest artist. She came to be a pivotal figure in my career.

We performed in the Melbourne season and then were given all the various travel documents like plane tickets and accommodation details to travel to Sydney to appear in *Spartacus* again with the company. Meanwhile, casting was announced for the next programs, including Graeme Murphy's *Beyond Twelve*. Both Steve and I were listed as understudies. Maggie had made it very clear that after the *Spartacus* seasons we would return to the school to complete our training. I was unsure what that meant. Did we have jobs in the company or was this just an extension of our secondment? I asked Steve anxiously: 'This is beyond *Spartacus*. Do you reckon we should say something?' He replied: 'Nup, let's just keep going,' and so we did. It seemed that while our names kept appearing on the noticeboard where casting announcements were made, our transition back to the school was put on hold. Then, thanks to an injury to a senior company dancer, I ended up dancing in the 'big nose' first cast with Kelvin and Paul de Masson, and my relationship with Kelvin started to take me to new, exciting and terrifying places. Steve and I kept being cast in all the repertoire, and so we continued touring.

Before long, the midyear break rolled around, and all the dancers had to have an interview with Maina. I mentioned to Maina that Steve and I seemed to have stayed in the company longer than intended and asked whether we ought to go back to the school. 'Oh no,' she replied briskly, 'you're in the company now.' And that was that. I was now a professional dancer with The Australian Ballet.

By the end of 1983, Steve and I were promoted to coryphée – the next level up from corps de ballet. My dad rang Maggie to see if

I would get a diploma from the school (perhaps still worrying about a fallback if the ballet ever fell through). Maggie explained that I could if I came back and did the final third-year exams, but there was no way I was going to do that. For a start, I had a job, the one I had always wanted. Secondly, our promotion had ruffled a few feathers at the school – I had a feeling that some of the teachers and students thought Steve and I were a bit full of ourselves because we were in the company. Perhaps we were, and they were right. I didn't want to go back to the school to face that.

My friendship with Darren became a little strained because of it, but thankfully this was resolved when he was given a job in the company at the end of his third year. We had begun that momentous year of 1983 by moving out of our respective homestays and into a flat together, because I was suddenly working and had more money than I'd ever had in my life. I was so used to living on $10 a week that by the end of the eight-week tour with The Dancers Company, I'd saved about $1200, all of which I stashed away in my bank account. Darren and I rented in Parkville, just a two-minute walk to the Ballet Centre. Though I was working, Darren was still a student without a substantial income, so we ended up sharing a bedroom with two single beds and we rented out the other bedroom to a first-year boy. With me away a lot on tour it worked out reasonably well, and Darren often had the room to himself.

It was the twenty-first anniversary of The Australian Ballet in 1983 and there were plenty of social functions to attend, some of them formal events organised by the company. The major celebration for the anniversary was a function at Leonda by the Yarra, to which I was given an invitation that read 'David and partner'. I assumed that meant I was supposed to bring a girl, so I made my first attempt at a date by inviting a friend from my first year, Delia Harrington. The evening wasn't the start of a grand romance, but we continued to be great friends, and I also got to know her warm and generous parents, Brenda and Ken.

Delia joined the school the same year I did, and was equally obsessive about ballet. We had been friendly during our time at the school and she was very excited when I was asked to join the company. Before we went back in 1983 – me to begin with the company and Delia in her third year – she invited me to lunch at her parents' house. Her mum had made a tuna casserole with crumbled Weet-Bix on top, which I thought was amazing and ate at least two helpings of. Also at the lunch was a friend of Delia's called Elizabeth – Lizzie – Toohey, a company dancer who had joined in 1980 and been the corps de ballet representative during the strike in 1981. With long auburn hair, a quick wit and confidence, Lizzie was a force of nature. We instantly became friends, and after lunch I agreed to help her move into her new apartment later that day.

This was the beginning of a friendship that became one of the most enduring and important in my life. Little did I know what lay in store for us, and it is rather funny now to look back and see that it all began with lifting boxes and tuna mornay.

CHAPTER 4

Maina and Lizzie

While my new friendship with Lizzie was bubbling away, my first year in the company was full of great excitement and major adjustments. A key one was getting to know the highly anticipated, much-talked-about new artistic director, Maina Gielgud, who arrived a few days after the start of the year.

I had met Maina before, in a role where I'd been trying (rather unusually) to make myself invisible. She had been in Melbourne the previous year as part of the interview process for the artistic director role, and at the time I was in the school while the company was performing Valentina and Leonid Kozlov's *The Nutcracker*. The Ballet Society held a small party for opening night, and we boys from the school were asked to be wine waiters. I was introduced to Maina by Noel Pelly, the assistant administrator, who was obviously looking after her during her visit. The name 'Gielgud' stuck in my head.

When it was finally announced that Maina had been appointed, we all remembered her from that night, and there was a lot of excitement about her arrival. Her CV was certainly impressive. The niece of the famous British actor Sir John Gielgud, Maina trained in London and Paris before joining France's Ballets de Roland Petit in 1961. She danced with several French companies, rising quickly through the ranks to become a *première danseuse* (principal) in 1963. She later danced with the Staatsoper Ballet Berlin, London Festival Ballet and Sadler's Wells Royal Ballet as a principal. In addition to all of that, she had been a guest artist with many companies around the world, including The Australian Ballet. She arrived in Melbourne with vast experience from a very cosmopolitan background. We junior dancers were suitably in awe of her – Steve Heathcote and I, still only on secondment with the company, expected to be returned to the school straight after *Spartacus*.

Maina made it clear the company would be run differently under her guidance. For a start, she did not want to be called 'Miss Gielgud' – as had been the tradition with artistic directors before her – but simply 'Maina'. It's hard to believe now, but at the time it was quite a controversial move in a company wedded to its traditions. And in keeping with this approach, Maina immediately set about dismantling the company's internal hierarchy, which had always been rigidly observed.

One of Maina's great attributes was that she was able to talk to anyone and everyone, always stopping to introduce herself. When my time finally came to meet Maina in her new role, it took a rather shocking turn. I was walking past her in the corridor one day when she stopped me and said: 'Oh, you're one of the new boys,' to which I said, 'Yes.'

'What's your name?' she asked.

'David,' I replied, to which she smiled and said, 'It's nice to meet you.' And then she studied me for just a moment before adding: 'Maybe we should think about a nose job.' I was gobsmacked. I didn't know what to say. I knew I had a pretty big nose, but I was taken aback that this was the first thing my new boss had observed in me. While I stood there trying to think of a reply, she added: 'Let's see what it looks like on stage,' and then she was gone.

With that sucker punch to deal with, I walked away, wondering if my nose was going to require surgical intervention. For the next few weeks, whenever Maina was in the room I made a great effort never to be seen in profile, so she wasn't alerted to my big honker – I became like a beacon in the night, constantly shining my face towards her. Eventually, to my enormous relief, we met again and this time, Maina gave my nose the all clear. 'Oh no, it's fine,' she said, and that was that.

Even though my nose had been waved through, it was nonetheless something I was always sensitive about. From time to time I did think about having a nose job – especially when a friend in the company had one that was exquisite and I was quite envious of it – but the timing never seemed right. I continued to advance through the ranks so it wasn't a serious concern, and then it was just too late and I had learnt to live with it.

It may seem shocking to modern sensibilities that an artistic director would make such a comment to a young dancer, but at the time it was completely normal – we were in an aesthetic profession, and what we looked like mattered. These days I wouldn't dream of saying such a thing to a dancer – I think the fact that I was never the male classical ballet ideal has made me much less concerned about what dancers look like and more interested in what they can do. Maina was, too – she was simply a forthright person who told it like it was.

Maina also shook the trees in other ways. Early in her tenure, she made it clear that casting would be on merit: 'In my mind, you're all dancers,' she said, 'and if a choreographer comes in and wants to put a corps de ballet girl with a principal boy then I think the choreographer gets their wish.' She did as she said she would, too – some of us youngsters were given great opportunities, but if a dancer didn't perform, they didn't get the plum roles, regardless of rank. This led to some controversial castings – especially when she elevated a younger dancer to a role while overlooking a more senior person. Maina was a very strong leader with a clear idea of how she wanted things to be, and an exacting one, too: she had a great capacity for hard work and expected all of us to be the same. It was Maina's way or the highway.

This style was not going to suit everyone, especially in a company that was still a little wary of management from the strike days. Maina enjoyed a honeymoon period for a few months, but then the rumblings began, with some of the dancers becoming ready to storm the barricades once again. There were meetings about what should be done and, as a seconded kid from the school who didn't even have an established place in the company, I found it all a bit nerve-racking – I didn't want there to be any trouble because I was having such a good time.

The ructions persisted for a long time – well after Maina's first year with the company and after I had signed a proper contract. To her credit, Maina always attended meetings with the dancers and fielded their questions – even if they didn't like her answers. Ultimately, she said, it was her job to make decisions that she believed were in the best interests of the company as a whole – it's a philosophy that stayed with me later when I took on that role.

Some of the dancers, particularly those in the more senior ranks, could see the writing on the wall, and left. Some were ready to retire, but a larger group had been schooled in the company's old ways, and this was too much change for them, or change they didn't like. The Australian Ballet in 1983 was still nursing a lot of wounds.

While all this was going on, Darren – who was in his final year at the school – was seconded to the company for a few productions and ended up dancing with Lizzie. He struck up a friendship with her, and because I was sharing a flat with Darren, my friendship with Lizzie continued to blossom, too – especially when her relationship with her fiancé ended and she sometimes spent the night on the couch in our living room to have a night away from the share house she was living in.

When we decided to turn in for the night, Darren and I would go into our twin-share bedroom and start singing songs from our favourite Marilyn Monroe cassette (featuring songs from her movies), to the great amusement of Lizzie in the living room. We would belt out 'Diamonds Are a Girl's Best Friend' and 'Heat Wave', but our absolute favourite was 'Two Little Girls from Little Rock' – I sang the Jane Russell part and Darren sang Marilyn's part. Over several years of night-time rehearsal we had perfected this, and it had become a bit of a party piece. Lizzie loved it and would laugh and laugh from the couch – a perfect lullaby!

At the end of 1983, Darren was offered a place in the company and decided to move out on his own, and the ballet school student who was sharing with us also wanted to leave – one Marilyn Monroe singalong too many, perhaps. Lizzie was looking for somewhere new to live, so it seemed an obvious fit: she moved in with me at the beginning of 1984. Two other dancers from the company, Glen Harris and Glen Murray, lived upstairs in the same apartment block, so there were lots of opportunities to have joint parties and dinners.

Lizzie brought with her 'Eunice', a cobalt blue Ford Laser, so we had the great luxury of access to a car to travel around in – and I was able to get a lift home after performances at the Palais most nights.

As the year went on, the four of us living in our apartment block realised that it was silly to be paying two sets of rent and utilities when we could just rent a house together. We spent one Saturday travelling around Melbourne's inner suburbs, clutching a copy of *The Age*'s rental listings. After just a day of looking, we all agreed on a single-fronted Victorian terrace in Falconer Street, North Fitzroy, and to our delight our application was accepted.

It was a fun house. Lizzie had the rather grand front bedroom, Glen Harris and I twin-shared the large middle room, and Glen Murray took the tiny third bedroom at the rear of the house. We had a lolly jar that was always full and a 'kitty' for groceries. Once again, it was a bit of a party house, and we'd often have people over for dinner. Sometimes we'd cook together, or if one of us had a night off, we'd cook dinner for the house. Mostly it worked really well – though I did have a disaster one night when I made a quiche for everyone to enjoy after that night's performance. I left it to cool on the bench while I went to collect the others from the theatre. When I returned home it was black with ants – a hard lesson in never leaving food out in that house.

Mostly we ate healthily, mindful of diet and the energy we all needed for our work, but sometimes we were on different nutritional paths. Glen Harris was always trying to gain weight and I was always trying to lose it; I worried about my solid thighs and didn't want them to get any bigger. He frequently made scrambled eggs for breakfast and, because he was a late riser, would eat them in the car on the way to work, while I just had fruit and then would look longingly at the scrambled eggs all the way to the Ballet Centre. (If only I'd known that the occasional egg was probably better for me!)

The women in the company were always under obvious pressure about their weight and shape, but the men were not spared, either. I was not tall and had always been bottom-heavy, with wide hips and strong, muscular thighs and calves, but a finer and weaker upper body. My legs did me a great service – they were the reason I was so good at jumps and turns. But I worried about how they looked, and whether they might reduce my chance of being cast as a prince – the holy grail for male classical dancers.

Unlike today, we had no idea about proper nutrition or the most suitable kind of diet for the work we were doing, so we just muddled along as best we could. It's not like the company or even ballet more generally was an outlier in this. It was the 1980s, and thin was in. Ballet had its own aesthetic on top of that: it wasn't enough to be thin – you had to be long as well. Your 'lines' – from your fingertips to the ends of your pointed toes – had to be long and beautiful, even if you were short. I was forever trying to lengthen my lines and divert attention away from my stockiness.

When I was in the ballet school, I returned home one summer holiday and visited our family doctor, who had been seeing me since I was a toddler, as I had a bout of bronchitis I was having trouble shifting. The doctor greeted me with: 'Oh my god, look at you! You've built a set of really good, strong footballer legs.' Although he meant it kindly, it was all I could do not to burst into tears on the spot. That comment became permanently etched in my brain.

Maina was very keen on thinness. The girls she favoured were very slender with long legs – dancers such as the lovely Christine Walsh – while the boys were tall and lean but muscular, like Greg Horsman and Steve Heathcote. I was very aware that I was neither thin nor long-legged, hence the confused diet and constant worry about my legs. At one stage I managed to catch a ferocious gastro bug and had to take three days off work, stricken with vomiting and diarrhoea. When I returned to work I was quite emaciated, having not eaten for several days, and Maina chirped, 'Oh, you look great!' That was The Look. Some of the dancers were even sent away to a place in Queensland to lose weight – again, at the time it was considered completely normal. (Years later, if I had done that as artistic director – perish the thought – it would not have been seen as a positive incentive but more like workplace harassment.)

I was so deeply, desperately in love with ballet that I would have done anything to achieve this physical ideal. In hindsight, I probably had a reasonably wholesome diet, but some of the dancers were doing quite unhealthy things to themselves in pursuit of thinness. Black coffee and cigarettes – indoor smoking was no problem in the 1980s, of course – were standard fare, as was a bit of drug-taking to boost energy and suppress appetite (although, in my usual way, I wasn't aware of it until much later).

I remember the first time someone offered me pseudoephedrine, because I was tired and we were all doing a lot of work. There were only sixty dancers in the company, and we were performing between 180 and 190 shows a year. The pace was furious, and the culture we worked in was that you went on stage no matter what. On this occasion, we were overseas, and I was deeply jet-lagged as well as generally exhausted. Someone gave me the 'cure-all' tablet and ... oh my god ... suddenly, I was invincible. I went and saw a show that I found *so* exciting, then we went to supper and I wasn't hungry, and then we did class, and, and, and ... Fortunately, I didn't have access to the pills myself, because I suspect I might have become hooked on them. After that one experience, my 'good boy' genes kicked in and I realised it wasn't a great idea. That was the end of that little dalliance.

Maina instilled, and insisted on, a work ethic that mirrored her own extraordinary drive. This meant that you did everything you could to avoid time off – it was seen as a weakness – so any physical ailments were masked with anti-inflammatories. I had had patellar tendonitis – a chronic inflammation around my knee – since my first year in the company, and recurrent ankle problems. But instead of doing strengthening exercises, which is really what would have been most beneficial (and what would be recommended today), I regularly mainlined anti-inflammatories so I could keep performing. I took anti-inflammatories fairly consistently for my first five years in the company, just to avoid missing a performance.

We became used to being tired – we had some days when we'd rehearse until 5.30 pm and then do a show that night. Our non-performance day started with class from 10.30 until 11.45 am (daily class is essential for dancers to work on technique, test injury recovery and stay in performance condition), then we'd have a fifteen-minute break and rehearse until 2.30 pm, followed by a lunchbreak for an hour and fifteen minutes (the extra fifteen minutes was for changing and going out to get food, as there was no canteen at the Flemington ballet centre), and return for more rehearsals in the afternoon, finishing about 6.30 pm. On a performance day, class began at 11 am, finished at 12.15 pm, and then we had the same fifteen-minute break, followed by rehearsals until 3 pm. We then had a break in the afternoon before heading to the Palais for the evening show. During non-performance weeks, we worked five days and had the weekends off; during performances, though, there was an 'optional' Saturday class, which for Maina was not optional – if you missed it, she'd come and find you.

Despite the rigour of life in the company, I was in heaven. And we didn't let a bit of tiredness stop us from partying, either. When we were in Sydney, for example, we'd head to a fellow corps de ballet dancer's house on Saturday nights after the show, where we'd watch videos, smoke dope (not really my thing) and eat junk food (which I was far too eager to partake in) until the wee hours. We'd then have Sunday to recover and be back at work on Monday morning.

My career seemed to be on a very promising trajectory, and Maina was always warm and kind to me. I think she liked my boundless enthusiasm for ballet, which I expressed in my constant leaping up and down the Ballet Centre corridors or in my tendency to *grand jeté* across the Flemington streets in peak-hour traffic. Despite this, there was a certain rigid aesthetic in the company at the time, and I didn't quite fit it the way other male dancers like Steve and Greg did.

Maina had regular one-on-one chats with the company dancers, and early in my career she dropped a bombshell in her straight-talking way. She was promoting me to coryphée, she said, adding some encouraging words about how well I was doing and that I had a good career ahead of me. And then she followed up with this: 'I don't see that you are a prince, but I feel that there are many roles you will excel in.' She outlined what was happening in the year ahead, highlighting Bim in *Gaîté Parisienne* as a role for a short, talented dancer. She didn't think I'd be in the triple bill featuring Glen Tetley's *Voluntaries* – a brilliant contemporary piece done in white lycra bodysuits, in which long lines are key. All I heard in this exchange was what I would *not* be doing, rather than what I would be doing, and my heart sank accordingly.

I came away a jumble of emotions: I was thrilled to be promoted, and so quickly, but crestfallen that Maina didn't see me as a prince. If she didn't see me as a prince, that meant she didn't see me as a principal, and that was a devastating realisation. But in the manner that has served me so well over the years, I worked through my initial disappointment and decided that there were all kinds of princes; I was simply going to prove her wrong. Or more precisely, given the fact she was my boss, change her mind.

I remembered reading an interview with Nureyev in which he said that he always believed that if he worked really hard, good things would happen. Even when he was growing up in a remote part of the Soviet Union, he always felt that someone would find him, and that hard work and talent would bring its eventual reward. This idea had resonated with me as a kid in Perth, where I had also felt isolated from the world I desperately wanted to be a part of. It had worked then, so I decided to stick with it.

And to a large extent, it succeeded. At the end of 1983, Maina chose me as one of seven dancers she referred to as the 'Christmas kids', who were given the amazing opportunity to travel to the United States and take classes with American Ballet Theatre, which at the time had in its ranks ballet superstars such as Mikhail Baryshnikov, Gelsey Kirkland and Natalia Makarova. Having grown up in Europe, Maina was acutely aware of our isolation in Australia – geographically and artistically – and the inhibiting effect it had on our artistic development, especially in those pre-internet days when you couldn't just jump online and watch a performance on YouTube. My fellow dancers chosen to be the very first 'Christmas kids' were Joady Chambers, Martyn Fleming, Greg Horsman, Lisa Pavane, Christopher Goldsworthy and Fiona Tonkin. We were all sent off to the United States, with the first stop being Washington, DC – it was my first time travelling outside of Australia and was an incredibly motivating adventure.

We were greeted in Washington by Wendy Walker, an expat Australian who was working as ballet mistress for American Ballet Theatre. By the time we arrived, we were almost demented with jet lag, kept awake only by the intense excitement of being able to visit one of the best ballet companies in the world. We took a class with the company at the Kennedy Center, and all the big stars were there – Baryshnikov, Makarova, Kirkland, along with their dogs in the classroom! Also in the class, which was packed, were Danilo (Danny) Radojevic and Ross Stretton, two well-known Australian principal dancers who had both begun their careers as members of The Australian Ballet and whom I came to know very well later in my career.

We were desperate to make a good impression in class, but we were also completely overwhelmed and exhausted. At the time, American Ballet Theatre was performing Baryshnikov's *Cinderella*, and we saw the performance that night. All I remember of it was that it featured men dancing *en pointe* as the Ugly Sisters, and another man in the company dancing as a dog and receiving a huge ovation at the end. We left Washington the next day and headed to New York, where we stayed across the road from Lincoln Center and saw New York City Ballet perform nearly every night. We saw *The Nutcracker* on New Year's Eve, with the conductor wearing a crazy blue feathered hat from *The Concert*, and Patricia McBride (one of the star ballerinas) dancing the Sugar Plum Fairy alongside Ib Andersen as the Prince. It was a memorable night. Afterwards, we went to the apartment of Ellen Zeisler, our company's New York representative who looked after our interests with local agents and kept us connected in the days before

Top left: Me in the backyard of our family home in Perth, Australia, 1965. My outfit is inspiration for a future costume worn in Stanton Welch's *Sylvia*. **Top right:** Wanting to be a 'ballet saint' at my First Holy Communion, 1970. **Bottom:** The McAllister siblings in our 70s Sunday best, all purple, paisley and big collars! Left to right: Phillip, me, Dianne, Paul and James (in Dianne's arms).

Top left: Standing by the old pool with my sister, Dianne, ready for dance class, 1973. **Top right:** Granny (Mum's mum) on the veranda, 1970s. She was one of the biggest early supporters of my ballet dreams. **Bottom left:** I could never just stand still in a photograph! Family and friends by the new backyard pool, with me doing a high kick, 1974. **Bottom right:** Princeling: a study in red on the way to the ballet studio in Cremorne Arcade, Perth, Australia, 1970s.

Giving 'attitude', having received honours for the Pre-Elementary Royal Academy of Dance exam, 1976.

Top left: Grinning and bearing it in my annual school photo, taken in the midst of tough school years, 1970s. **Top right:** Couldn't miss an opportunity to play to the camera. On the family road trip to the eastern states, about to jump into the Holden Premier, 1979. (Phillip McAllister/personal collection) **Bottom:** A family shot from our trip east, Cooks' Cottage, Melbourne, Australia, 1979. Left to right: Dad, Dianne, James, Mum, Paul and me. (Phillip McAllister/personal collection)

Top: Di came to visit and got to see my 'bold and beautiful' bedroom, Moonee Ponds, Melbourne, Australia, 1981. **Bottom:** Striking poses during the Sydney season at the flat I shared with Darren Spowart, April 1984. (Dianne McAllister/personal collection)

Top: Dancing with Kathy Downey in my very first professional performance, Geelong Performing Arts Centre, Vic., Australia, 1982. (Liz King/personal collection)
Bottom: Pre-show preparation in my dressing room at the Sydney Opera House, Australia, 1983.

Top left: *Beyond Twelve* in 1983: the only time I enjoyed wearing football gear. (Branco Gaica) **Top right:** Look, Mum: no hands! Performing the pas de deux from *Le Corsaire* for the Fifth International Ballet Competition at the Bolshoi Theatre, Moscow, Russia, 1985. (Alexander Chernykh/personal collection) **Bottom:** Posing for post-class snaps with the famous Russian teacher Asaf Messerer at the Bolshoi Theatre, 1985. Left to right: Elizabeth Toohey, Asaf Messerer, Kelvin Coe and me. (Dally Messenger)

Top: Bronze-medal winner, fashion victim! On stage at the medal presentation ceremony for the Fifth International Ballet Competition, Bolshoi Theatre, 1985. (Alexander Chernykh/personal collection) **Bottom:** Flying high with Elizabeth Toohey in Walter Bourke's *Grand Tarantella* at the Palais Theatre, Melbourne, Australia, 1985. (Robert McFarlane, courtesy of Josef Lebovic Gallery, Sydney)

Playing Mr Smithers in Robert Ray's *The Sentimental Bloke* – always SO successful with the ladies! Left to right: Peta Davidson, Miranda Coney, me, Susan Elston and Elizabeth Toohey at the Sydney Opera House's Joan Sutherland Theatre, 1985. (Branco Gaica)

Top left: Sitting in rehearsal with a ballet legend at the Bolshoi Theatre, during the first return visit to Moscow in 1986. Left to right: Maya Plisetskaya, Elizabeth Toohey (in the mirror) and me. **Top right:** We're back! Me and Elizabeth Toohey in front of the Bolshoi Theatre during our return trip in 1987. **Bottom:** Performing in Harald Lander's *Études*, 1986 – one of my favourite solos. Left to right: Miranda Coney, Tanya Rhodes, Joady Chambers, me, Margaret Illmann, Ulrike Lytton and Michele Goullet. (David Parker)

Top left: Dancing with Steven Heathcote (upstage) in Graeme Murphy's *Gallery*, 1987 – one of the many magical moments I shared with Steve on stage. (David Simmonds) **Top right:** Caught in a quad stretch while getting ready for rehearsal at a ballet studio in Tbilisi, Georgia, 1988. (Elizabeth Toohey/personal collection) **Bottom:** Wearing too much make-up to meet the Queen? Left to right: me, Elizabeth Toohey, Colin Peasley, Hugh Colman, Maina Gielgud and Her Majesty Queen Elizabeth II after the performance of Maina Gielgud's *The Sleeping Beauty* in Covent Garden, London, England, 1988. (Desmond O'Neill)

Top left: Tongue-tied with Princess Diana after the Royal Gala performance of *Coppélia* in London, England, 1992. Left to right: me, Miranda Coney, Maina Gielgud and Diana, Princess of Wales. (Ronald G Bell/The Australian Ballet archive) **Top right:** Still dancing in the streets, even in China. Great Wall of China, 1993. (Jim McFarlane) **Bottom:** Going for gold! Promotional shot for Glen Tetley's *Gemini*, 1991. (Jim McFarlane)

Top: 'Here's looking at you, kid.' Rolling in the hay with Fiona Tonkin in Sir Frederick Ashton's *La Fille mal gardée*, 1989. (David Simmonds) **Bottom left:** Getting physical with Vicki Attard in a studio shot for Stephen Baynes's *El Tango*, 2000. (Greg Barrett) **Bottom right:** Making beautiful shapes with Madeleine Eastoe in Graeme Murphy's *The Nutcracker*, 2000. (Branco Gaica)

Top: Caught in the act creating my 2015 version of *The Sleeping Beauty* in the studio. Left to right: Robyn Hendricks, Rina Nemoto, Nicola Curry, me and Natasha Kusen. (Kate Longley) **Bottom:** Robyn Hendricks and Daniel Gaudiello in *Dyad 1929* by Wayne McGregor, 2009 – one of the many exciting commissioned ballets of my tenure as artistic director. (Jim McFarlane)

Top: Everyone needs a fairy godmother! Left to right: Ingrid Gow, Sarah Thompson, Dimity Azoury (kneeling in front), Amy Harris, Sharni Spencer and Dana Stephensen in *The Sleeping Beauty*, 2017. (Kate Longley) **Bottom:** A classic 'gotcha' moment. Top to bottom: Christopher Rodgers-Wilson, Benedicte Bemet and me in Ronald Hynd's *The Merry Widow*, 2018. (Kate Longley)

Top: Fun in the sun at my last photo shoot for The Australian Ballet, Broken Hill, NSW, Australia, 2019. Left to right: Callum Linnane, Dimity Azoury, Robyn Hendricks, me, Valerie Tereshchenko and Jake Mangakahia. (Georges Antoni) **Bottom:** Wesley Enoch and me, newly in love at the 2008 Australian Dance Awards, Arts Centre Melbourne, Australia. (Julie Dyson)

the internet, and watched the famous ball drop at Times Square while eating ten different kinds of bagel (who knew such things existed?). Later, Julie da Costa, a distinguished senior soloist in the company whom I had been lucky enough to dance with a few times in my first year, and her entertainer fiancé, Daryl Somers, invited us to a party at The Plaza, which was incredibly swanky. They were holidaying in New York and Daryl was catching up with his contacts there. It was extremely generous of them to invite us to their very stylish party. We were still jet-lagged: I remember Julie saying later that we arrived looking like 'space cadets'.

While we were in New York, we saw a lot of performances of works by world-renowned choreographers Jerome Robbins and George Balanchine, and it was this exposure that led me to fall ardently in love with the Balanchine repertoire. I had never seen New York City Ballet; I'd only heard of them and the works of founder George Balanchine. It was fabulous to see the company at this time, especially as Balanchine had only just died, so the dancers, who were great stars, were still dancing in the ballets he created for them. There was such life and vigour in their dancing. They were all fearless and danced with incredible speed and precision. Everything I had heard about this company and choreographer came to life in these awe-inspiring performances; I knew that this was a style of dancing I wanted to see more of and dance myself.

After New York, we flew to Toronto, where we watched rehearsals and took classes with The National Ballet of Canada. It was a flying visit and the company wasn't performing, but we did get to meet superstar Erik Bruhn, who had been The Australian Ballet's first-ever guest artist in 1962. It was a wonderful experience and the company dancers were extremely friendly and welcoming.

We then travelled back to the Big Apple for a final week, taking classes with the revered teacher David Howard. We saw musicals at Times Square, including *My One and Only*, starring Twiggy and Tommy Tune, and the first season of *Dreamgirls*, after which we then – in a very New York kind of way – met some of the performers at a cafe next door following the show. We were also taken to see a rehearsal at the Dance Theatre of Harlem – just getting there was an experience in itself. At the time, Harlem was in the grip of drug wars and completely off limits to young tourists like us. A car was arranged to pick us up and collect us after the rehearsal, and there were people at the studios to greet us when we arrived. It was brilliant watching such an innovative, exciting company rehearse, but it was also an extraordinary insight into how different a city could be in the short distance of a few streets.

Our amazing North American journey came to an end, but we had one more thing we wanted to do before flying home: a stopover in Los Angeles to go to Disneyland. After all the high culture we'd experienced, it was huge fun to let our inner children run free for the day before catching a flight to Sydney.

Back home after such a heady trip that had opened my eyes and taught me so much, my career continued to develop. By the end of 1983, I had danced Mercutio in *Romeo and Juliet* and a soloist part in *Tales of Hoffmann*. What's more, when renowned choreographer Glen Tetley arrived in Melbourne in 1984 to teach us *Voluntaries*, he insisted on doing his own casting, and I was cast, despite my earlier disappointment following the chat with Maina.

The first thing the dancers do in *Voluntaries* is a *présage* lift overhead – the boy lifts the girl, who is *en pointe* in an arabesque position, straight up over his head, with arms fully extended (it is sort of the ballet equivalent to a 'clean and jerk'). It requires enormous strength and control to do well. I had never done a *présage* on stage and I was terrified. The two Glens (my housemates) felt the same way – we were the 'dancey' boys, not the 'lifty' boys.

As well as being a famous choreographer, Glen Tetley was an inspirational teacher, and as it turned out he would become a great supporter of mine throughout my career, for which I am eternally grateful. He wanted not just lifters but dancers. *Voluntaries* contained a difficult, showy boys' dance with a cabriole entrance – scissoring the legs to meet each other while jumping. I could do that, which is why I was cast, and fortunately the partnering, which I was still slightly anxious about, came with a great deal of practice. Scott Douglas, Glen's partner and the ballet master for the show, spent months with us working on those *présages*. While the partnering was really tough, we never missed one in any of our performances. This was a real turning point in terms of my partnering, which until that stage I'd viewed as a weakness. With hard work, I realised that I could in fact be a very good partner, and after this experience I felt much more confident.

Later in the year, we started working on Maina's production of *The Sleeping Beauty*, the big production for the year. With Maina there were always a lot of casts, and I was in the fifth cast for the Bluebird pas de deux, which meant there were four other dancers going on stage before me – in other words, I was way down in the 'batting order'. The Bluebird pas de deux was a wonderful, show-offy, technically difficult exhibition piece in Act III. I was partnered with Fiona Tonkin, with whom I had performed a number of roles that year. She was a senior artist (one step below principal) so I was paired well above my pay rate. As we were doing camera rehearsals for the simulcast to be shown live on the ABC, Joady Chambers (a soloist who was also dancing the Bluebird pas de deux in a cast ahead of Fiona and me) injured her foot and couldn't dance, which meant Fiona was shunted up to dance with Greg Horsman. Lizzie, who was also doing the pas de deux in another cast, was then moved up to partner with me. We had to rehearse on the Sunday before the performance because the timing was so tight and we were down for one of the early shows in the run.

Partnerships in ballet, a bit like in life, are mercurial things. Sometimes they click and are brilliant; sometimes, for no clear reason, they fall a little flat. When they do fall flat, it's likely because you and your partner do not have a shared outcome, and you are going about the performance differently. It can be extremely difficult to deal with, and I was lucky that this only happened to me a couple of times in my career.

It's hard to say why Lizzie and I clicked the way we did, and it was probably for a whole range of reasons. For a start, even though we had rarely danced together – I was usually paired with Fiona – we knew each other extremely well as friends and housemates. Thrown together at the last minute and having to learn Bluebird very quickly, the chemistry between us was immediate and noticeable not just to us, but those watching. With its fast pace and demanding choreography, a successful Bluebird pas de deux really hangs on the synchronicity between the two dancers. Lizzie and I shared a strong musicality, which meant we heard the music in the same way, and this made it very easy to dance together.

Sometimes partnerships are also about being a good physical fit – about being the right height for each other. That said, strong partnering should be able to offset any height difference. The harmony is really more about sharing a particular style of dancing, and this was certainly the case for Lizzie and me – we were able to bring out the best in each other on stage. We were both good at jumps, and 'bravura' dancing – the spectacular, show-offy stuff – was also a great asset to our partnership.

Later in our careers, we needed other dancers to help us develop different aspects of our performance and in turn enable us to do a wider range of ballets. For example, Lizzie was wonderful in *The Taming of the Shrew* as Kate, but I would never have been a convincing Petruchio. Similarly, dancing with Fiona Tonkin in ballets like *The Sleeping Beauty* and *La Fille mal gardée* allowed me to be more romantic on stage, as Fiona was smaller than I was (even when she was *en pointe*) and very feminine in her performances. To be honest, I think what really made Lizzie and me exciting to watch was that it was always a competition – we loved to come out on stage and try to outdo each other. It made for great viewing for the audience and, fortunately for us, did not result in injury.

At any rate, it was a partnership that attracted a lot of attention. Two months later, we were packing up and heading for Sydney to perform *The Sleeping Beauty*. By this stage, Glen Murray had decided to leave the company and our Falconer Street house. My dear mate Darren had taken a job with Sydney Dance Company, so he was looking for a permanent living arrangement in the harbour city. Usually, if the company was touring in Sydney, Darren and I took short-term accommodation together, so this left me without a flatmate for the tour. Lizzie then kindly offered for me to stay with her at her sister Helen's apartment in Bellevue Hill – and with great relief, I accepted.

Lizzie and I had become extremely close, enhanced by the success of our Bluebird pairing. I was not dating anyone. To my way of thinking, I had never actually dated anyone; not in an open way that you might call a relationship. As you've seen, throughout 1983 my friendship with Kelvin had developed into what I found to be an uncertain, exciting and slightly terrifying romantic relationship. Kelvin clearly wanted us to be a couple and be open about our relationship, but I was not ready for that. I still desperately wanted to be 'normal', and to me that meant being straight. I could not come to terms with the idea that what those schoolyard bullies had said about me all those years ago might be true – that I was a 'poofter', a 'pansy'. Because I had so much difficulty coming to terms with this in my own mind, I pushed it to one side and instead allowed my obsession with ballet to be all-consuming.

Kelvin – kind, gentle and wise – was a ballet role model as well as a great friend. I loved watching him dance and longed to be able to do the things he could do on stage. Our initial furtive romantic liaison slowly became more of a regular thing – but it was very much under the radar. We were dancing together and sleeping together, and as far as I knew, no one in the company was aware of it – or if they were, they didn't let on. At work, I was happily cultivating an image of mystery (sexually at least – in terms of ballet, I was a wide-open book). I didn't want to be seen as one of the 'gay boys' and so I did not come out – mostly because I hadn't yet accepted it in my own mind and wouldn't for many more years. I was also still young and very naive, and all I wanted to do was compartmentalise my life: be a total 'bun head', as we used to say, while at work, and then be whatever I wanted in my life outside of work, without labels.

Towards the end of 1983, Kelvin could see I wasn't coping – and honestly, it wasn't fair to him. I didn't want to be in a relationship with him, but I kept willingly jumping into his bed. He generously gave me a way out by telling me I needed to go away and sort myself out. I gratefully took it. After that I did my usual trick of burying myself in work.

Then, along came Lizzie.

At the flat in Bellevue Hill, there was only one bedroom with a double bed – this was not especially noteworthy, as we'd shared a bed platonically before. But this time it was different, and after a show one night, we became lovers. It was a rush of excitement and uncertainty – I'd never so much as kissed, much less made love to, a woman before. I felt like my heart was going to burst.

The next morning, I ate mango for the first time. I remember it vividly because, growing up in Perth in the 1960s and 70s, we did not have access to such exotic delights, except perhaps in a can (which I also don't recall ever tasting). Even now I still associate mangoes with this extraordinary time in my life. Those were heady days! A successful dance partnership, tropical fruits and, finally, wonderfully, a girlfriend. A girlfriend! I could have shouted it from the rooftops. I was about to turn twenty-one, life was grand, and for the first time I felt completely *normal*.

Unfortunately, in the excitement and newness of it all, I didn't handle my altered life status particularly well, leading to a difficult weekend with my family. My whole family had travelled over from Perth for my twenty-first and were staying at a hotel on Manly Beach. They were coming to see Lizzie and me perform Bluebird at the

Sydney Entertainment Centre on my actual birthday. However, I was not happy with our performance that night and so was in a funk when we all went to a restaurant near the theatre for supper afterwards. The atmosphere was very tense. I told my sister about Lizzie, and then my parents. But rather than being thrilled, as I expected they would be, they were strangely hostile, especially my mum. I think, in hindsight, that I was just so thrilled to be in this relationship that I had become completely wrapped up in it. Mum, who never liked surprises, felt she'd been blindsided. I was the first of her sons to introduce a girlfriend to the family, and it was all something of a shock. A party my parents had organised that weekend to celebrate my birthday was similarly tense, and the whole trip was a bit of a disaster.

Eventually the tension dissolved and we fell back into our usual rhythms. By the time I returned to Perth at Christmas, all had been forgiven, and my parents became used to me spending a lot of time on the phone to Newcastle (where Lizzie was from). I was also focused on getting my driver's licence, as Lizzie was tired of being the sole driver in our household. I managed to achieve this on my last day in Perth, which was a huge relief as I was terrified of having to take the driving test in Melbourne, with all the traffic, tramlines and weird hook turns.

It was joyous to return to Melbourne after the Christmas break and be back with Lizzie. We were by now both soloists, dancing together and sleeping together. I moved into the front bedroom at Falconer Street with Lizzie and tried my best to be a good boyfriend – though, honestly, I had no idea what I was doing sometimes, and having such limited experience with women, I felt a little like I was searching in the dark. I also found I had very few male friends I could turn to for advice on relationship matters, and in the absence of the internet, I just had to muddle through as best I could.

During this time many dancers were given nicknames, and I was a little disappointed that I had never been interesting enough to be 'christened' with one. This all changed the next time the company was performing in Perth. Lizzie came home with me on that trip, and in the process gave me a nickname that has stuck. My mum never liked to call me 'Dave' or 'Davey' or 'Davo' or any of the usual derivatives of David. But she sometimes called me 'Daze', and one day asked 'Where's Daze?' in front of Lizzie, who in turn made the short step from 'Daze' to 'Daisy'. And that was that. From then on, everyone in the company called me 'Daisy'. Finally I had my own nickname, which I embraced wholeheartedly.

Professionally, the chemistry Lizzie and I had created on stage continued to pay dividends. Towards the end of 1984, Maina told us that she'd like to send us to Moscow to compete in the Fifth International Ballet Competition. The competition is sort of like the Olympics of the ballet world. It was a bolt out of the blue. I don't think either of us had any hope that we would be the ones chosen to represent the company, as there was so much talent in our ranks at the time. It confirmed that Maina was happy with our performances and had noticed the spark we had on stage. The fact that this happened just as our romantic relationship was taking off was an added bonus and it certainly made me more confident to take on such a huge challenge. At that time, I felt that together we could achieve anything, even in the exotic ballet mecca of Moscow, where some of the greatest dancers in the world had come from. We were going to be among them.

We knew we had a lot of work to do, as the competition was in June the next year; we would have to train hard to be as polished as possible before competing. At the same time, we would still be performing with the company. Walter Bourke, a former Australian Ballet principal dancer and well-known restaurateur, gave us permission to perform his *Grand Tarantella*, which he had choreographed for himself and his ballerina wife, Maria. Most ballet competitions are made up of set repertoire that is standard, but to show your individuality you also present a piece that is 'unique' to each performer. We would perform Walter's *Grand Tarantella* in this round, when we could dance whatever we pleased. We were delighted, as it was extraordinary. The only downside was that as Walter was very busy with his restaurant, the only time we could rehearse was on a Sunday; this meant Lizzie and I had to work seven days a week for two months straight to get ready. I didn't mind one bit: I was young and fit and up for any challenge. Having Lizzie by my side as well made me feel invincible.

CHAPTER 5

To Moscow, in love

Lizzie and I heading to Moscow to compete was perfect media fodder: a pair of young dancers who were also in love. The weeks leading to our departure were a whirlwind of events, as the company organised interview after interview, and an all-in press call at which we danced a bit of the *Grand Tarantella*.

The general manager, Noel Pelly, who as a former publicist always had a keen eye for a publicity opportunity, made sure the company did not repeat the mistake it made in 1977, when Danny Radojevic won a gold medal at the International Ballet Competition – a remarkable achievement – but it barely registered as newsworthy back in Australia because the company didn't make much of a fuss about it. Not long after that, Danny joined American Ballet Theatre and became a principal. The Australian Ballet wisely wanted to make sure nothing like that happened again.

The competition was a knockout in three rounds, so we needed to prepare three pas de deux plus one 'free round' selection. We prepared four dances in total in the knowledge that if we were knocked out, we wouldn't get to dance them all. The Bluebird pas de deux from

The Sleeping Beauty was to be our first dance, as we'd already attracted so much positive attention from dancing it with the company, and we knew it well. Our second-round dance was from *La Fille mal gardée* – a technically challenging piece and one in a demi-character mould with strong, lively acting that suited both of us more than a highly romantic prince-and-his-love routine. Walter's *Grand Tarantella* – fast, difficult and spectacular if danced well – was our free round choice, and finally, our third-round pas de deux was from *Le Corsaire*. I thought *Corsaire* was a risky choice – I would have been much happier with a showy pas de deux from *Don Quixote* or even something from Vasily Vainonen's *Flames of Paris*, but we didn't know either of those pas de deux at the time. So *Corsaire* it was, and we set about rehearsing in our own time – lunchbreaks, evenings and weekends.

We worked like dogs. Any dancers who were envious of us being chosen for the Russian trip might have changed their minds when, night after night, we were still rehearsing long after they had gone home. Not that we minded – I felt like I was standing on the precipice of the Ballet Big Time. An additional benefit was getting to know Walter and Maria Bourke, who by this stage were at the height of their success running their restaurant in Carlton, called Maria and Walter's, which they had opened after retiring from being principal dancers. It's extraordinary to think about how they could manage both running a fine-dining restaurant and rehearsing us, but they were no strangers to hard work. The four of us met on Sundays and did a class together, and then we would rehearse the *Grand Tarantella* for an hour or two. After that we'd all go back to the restaurant or their home and Walter would cook us a magnificent lunch. We became extremely close with the Bourkes, and I remember this as a kind of 'family' time – they were incredibly supportive. When we were performing, Walter always said 'drop in on your way home', and so we would, often not arriving until about 10 pm. He would still make us a delicious meal paired with a glass of fantastic red wine.

Just before we left for Moscow, Maina asked Kelvin to be our coach for the competition, which meant he would travel with us, take care of us on the trip and oversee our final rehearsals for the pas de deux that we would perform. This seemed an inspired choice as Kelvin had himself been a silver medallist in the competition and had also coached Danny Radojevic when he won gold in 1977 dancing Walter's *Superboy*, another hugely successful bravura solo work that he had crafted especially for Danny.

The time came for us to depart, and we jetted off in June with high hopes and big plans – as well as a very challenging repertoire to perform. I was in seventh heaven: I had Kelvin with us, whom I trusted and admired and with whom I had shared so much, and my love sitting alongside me. We were determined to wow the audiences in Moscow.

We soon realised we were on the flight from hell. We flew from Melbourne to Sydney, then Sydney to Singapore, Singapore to Bombay, Bombay to Rome and then Rome to Vienna. We stayed in Vienna for three days, just about delirious from jet lag, in order to recover and prepare for the final leg to Moscow. There we took classes with the Staatsballett, rehearsed our pas de deux and caught up with some friends of Lizzie's. We even had time for a lunch in the Vienna woods. It was a welcome break in the journey, working in the beautiful city of Vienna, rehearsing in the Opera House where we were surrounded by European ballet stars. We felt we were living a very glamorous life indeed.

It became a little less glamorous when we opened the suitcase containing our costumes to give them an airing after the long flight, and discovered that somewhere along the line some customs officials had taken exception to the costume jewellery I was to wear for *Le Corsaire*, and confiscated most of it. This was baffling, but also a disaster in terms of our performance, so we had to go to the Austrian equivalent of a $2 shop and buy a gold scarf, elastic, a handful of tacky beads, a feather and a plastic brooch so that I could cobble together something resembling *Corsaire* jewels using Lizzie's pointe shoes sewing kit. All those days I sat as a kid alongside my mum while she sewed came in handy, and by the end of our time in Vienna I had some very serviceable jewellery to wear on stage.

Finally, we arrived in Moscow, where all the competitors were accommodated in the massive Rossiya Hotel in Red Square, which had three thousand rooms and could house more than four thousand guests. As a couple, Lizzie and I were allowed to share a room, providing we could actually find it. Every entrance to this monolith looked the same, so we spent quite some time walking around looking for the right way to our room. Each morning we'd see fellow dancers gathering for breakfast, which was basically black bread, boiled eggs and perhaps some cheese. Lizzie and I both lost a lot of weight during our stay in Moscow as the heavy cuisine didn't agree with us.

The day after we arrived and registered, there was a grand and star-filled opening night gala at the magnificent Bolshoi Theatre, where the competition would be staged during the day and then cleared away at night to allow the Bolshoi Ballet to perform.

The jury was revealed on stage and was made up of a 'who's who' of world ballet: the president of the competition was the legendary Yuri Grigorovich, the artistic director of the Bolshoi. The renowned choreographer Robert Joffrey (founder of the Joffrey Ballet) was its vice-president. There was a host of superstars on the jury, including Russian ballerina Galina Ulanova and Cuban ballet legend Alicia Alonso. To our great delight, Dame Margaret Scott was also on the jury as the Australian representative, which meant we had at least someone in our corner.

The competition was massive, with over one hundred competitors in the first round, to be spread over four days. Lizzie and I were scheduled to perform on day two, so we were sent to rehearse in the building where the Bolshoi's school was housed, which was like a ballet factory: dozens and dozens of studios in which competitors were assigned to rehearse. While we had all our music on cassettes, there were actually no cassette players, so we ended up having to rehearse to Kelvin singing the music, which was a little weird.

Russian audiences took a little getting used to as well. They left you in no doubt as to how they felt about you. Lizzie and I had made a pact not to watch any of the other competitors in case it unnerved us, but in the first round directly before we were to perform for the first time, a South American couple was greeted with such loud cheers by the crowd that my curiosity got the better of me. Thinking they must have been amazing, I took a peek and realised the audience wasn't actually applauding, but mocking – they were a knowledgeable crowd, and merciless towards any performances they didn't feel were up to scratch. They actually laughed out loud if they thought you were bad, as well as whistled and jeered. And if you were passable but not brilliant, they clapped politely, which was its own kind of damnation and a blow to your confidence. Realising this, I thought: *all we can do is go out there, dance up a storm and hopefully entertain them.*

By the time Lizzie and I had our chance to dance Bluebird, there had already been a lot of couples dancing the grand pas de deux from *The Sleeping Beauty*, so when our selection was announced there was an audible groan from the audience. Not a good reaction, I realised as I stood in the wings, already pulsing with nerves and adrenalin as I prepared to step out onto the world-famous Bolshoi stage for the very first time. Would it be the last? Then the first notes of the Bluebird pas de deux started and there was an obvious and overwhelming sense of relief from the crowd, glad they did not have to see another Prince and Aurora. We danced well, with energy and dynamism, and we pulled off all the tricky bits. Our final coda was exhilarating, the challenging diagonal steps together were perfectly synchronised; we were dancing completely as one with the music and left the stage having given it our all. We received a warm ovation and felt very pleased with our performance. The next day we started rehearsing hard for *La Fille mal gardée*, not yet knowing if we'd made it through to the second round, as there were still two more days of the first round to go.

Every night of the competition we were allowed to watch, in seats set aside for the competition dancers, the Bolshoi Ballet perform. This meant we were lucky enough to see one of the world's great companies perform *Raymonda*, *The Nutcracker* and *Spartacus*. There weren't enough seats for all the competitors each night, so it was always a bit of a crapshoot to get in. One particular night, however, Lizzie and I had no trouble finding seats and thought it strange that the competitors' section was so empty – it turned out all the other dancers were in the Tchaikovsky Foyer, the magnificent anteroom where we had chosen our competition numbers on the first day, to find out who had made it through to the second round. Between Act I and II that night, we discovered that we were among those who had successfully made it through, and we were thrilled.

The second round moved a lot faster, as half the contestants had been eliminated from the competition – there were now only about fifty dancers left. We were given fifteen-minute allocations to rehearse on stage – not the main stage, but on an almost identical one upstairs. By this time, Lizzie and I were tired and frazzled – our nerves were constantly being jangled by the excitement of performing and the anxiety of the competition. The night before we were to dance the second round, we were sniping at each other and things were generally tense. And then they got more so. During rehearsals for the *Grand Tarantella* – which we had to perform on the same day as the *La Fille mal gardée* pas de deux – Lizzie hit her calf hard with her pointe shoe midway through a jump and corked the muscle. We weren't having a useful rehearsal anyway, with both of us fatigued and cranky, and this seemed like the last straw. Lizzie was in tremendous pain and we worried that this meant the end of the competition for us. Maggie Scott happened to be watching this final rehearsal and was of great help to us, running around and fussing and trying to find ways to mend poor Lizzie's calf. With Maggie's help, Lizzie was taken to a fairly rudimentary medical clinic at the theatre and given ice, some kind of poultice and a bottle with a mysterious fluid in it that she was told to use to treat the injury. Kelvin and I took her back to our hotel room, but the tension surrounding all three of us was still great, so he and I went to watch the Bolshoi that night and left Lizzie to nurse her calf with all her potions. By the time we returned, she was asleep.

One of the things I really appreciated and loved about Kelvin was that, despite our past, he never said anything negative to me about my relationship with Lizzie. He no doubt suspected it wouldn't last long, but in spite of that, he never made comments – snide or otherwise. He was very fond of us both and seemed genuinely happy for us. He was a wise soul as well as a kind one, and his friendship and mentoring continued to mean the world to me.

The next morning, I woke wondering how it was all going to go – would Lizzie be able to dance, and were we even still speaking to each other? What was in that mysterious bottle of fluid she was dutifully applying? Mercifully, she was much improved, so much so that she declared herself able to perform that day. We completed a class and warmed up, and the muscle seemed okay – it felt like she'd had a miraculous recovery.

Amazingly, we danced our *Fille* pas de deux extremely well, greeted by thunderous applause at the end of it – the Russians seemed to particularly appreciate that we tackled the one-handed lift in the coda, which is basically the male lead holding his partner over his head with one hand under her bum. It's an exceptionally difficult but spectacular lift. Obviously it is great if you can pull it off, and we did. After the interval, we had to quickly regroup and dance the *Grand Tarantella*. It was exhausting, but we danced it as well as we ever had in any of the rehearsals, and we received five or six curtain calls, so overwhelming was the ovation. It was one of the great, triumphant days of our careers, made even more so by the tension and drama that had been circling around us the day before.

We were so relieved and thrilled that we bought some vodka to celebrate back in our room, but we had nothing to mix it with, so we grabbed a bottle of an unfamiliar orange, syrupy drink to offset the vodka's strength. Maggie, who had experienced the halted preparation the day before, joined Kelvin, Lizzie and me in our room to celebrate, and made a point of telling us we shouldn't have anything to drink because we might get through to the third round. Kelvin, ever the co-conspirator, filled up our glasses with this hideous orange cordial, and then sloshed in a liberal dose of vodka on the sly, avoiding Maggie's wrath and enabling us to have a very relaxing, slightly festive, evening.

By the end of the next night, we learnt we had made it through to the third and final round. The whole way through the competition, Lizzie and I kept saying to Kelvin: 'Oh, we probably won't make it through,' the classic way of pre-empting crushing disappointment. This annoyed Kelvin, so now he said to us sternly: 'Okay, you've made it through to the third round, so now you've got to stop talking yourselves down and be really confident.' Trouble was, *Le Corsaire* was our weakest pas de deux, and we all knew that, so we worked extremely hard on it for the next couple of days.

The third round left just twenty-four competitors performing over two evenings – in this round of the competition, dancers performed with an orchestra, not taped music, and it was televised. It was a big deal. The conductor had a lot of pieces to learn and twenty-four dancers he had never seen perform before. It was a daunting task to get every tempo just as each of us wanted, and to deal with all the choreographic subtleties of every competitor with only one rehearsal. It was quite uneven at times, with some strained smiles on stage as we watched the other competitors growing frustrated with timing and music. When our turn came, we danced *Le Corsaire* the best we'd ever performed it, but in spite of this, the ovation we had received and the headiness we had felt following the second-round performance could not be matched. After we danced, someone observed to me: 'You know, if the competition had finished after the second round, you'd probably have won gold medals.' By this stage, our exhaustion was such that it allowed us to be philosophical. We'd done the best we could; we'd made it to the final round and acquitted ourselves well. There was nothing more to be done. After more than a month of travel and performance, we had not been sent home and were relieved it was all finally over, satisfied we had performed as well as we had.

There was another day of competition and then a party to celebrate its conclusion. The morning after the competition's end, we received an early phone call asking us if we would like to dance the *Grand Tarantella* at the prize-giving gala. Being asked to dance meant we had won something – so there was huge excitement – but what? We were absolutely exhausted and sore: the tops of my feet were grazed and I sported rather impressive scabs to the insteps, where the first point of contact was made with the floor on landing on one knee from double *tours en l'air* (my favourite spinning jump) on a wooden stage, which had also led to bloodied tights and shredded skin. After five weeks in Russia and not particularly taking to the local cuisine, we were skinny and drained as well. We asked Kelvin if we could do a slightly shortened version of the *Grand Tarantella* for the gala, and he agreed.

At the medal presentation, I wore a very 1980s oversized Stuart Membery suit, which made me look like a kid wearing his dad's clothes. In our category, there were two gold medals, four silver and six bronze, shared between the men and women – strangely they awarded them not to couples but to individuals. I won a bronze medal and Lizzie won a special award for artistic merit. I was thrilled, but we were so exhausted that we didn't stay for the whole performance after the medal presentation. We danced in the first half of the performance and then headed back to the hotel for a quick supper with Kelvin and Maggie.

Just as we were about to go to bed, there was a knock at the hotel door. A big burly security guy and Yuri Grigorovich were standing there, a pretty terrifying sight late at night. 'There's been a mistake, you must come for supper,' Mr Grigorovich said, to which we of course agreed – what else could we do in the circumstances? – and hurried to get dressed again. We headed downstairs, where two black limousines were waiting for us. Puzzled and a little scared, Lizzie rang Kelvin before we departed and said, with some theatricality: 'I think we're being taken away by the KGB. If we're not here in the morning, ring the embassy.'

We needn't have worried. The editor-in-chief of the Communist Party newspaper *Pravda*, Viktor Afanasyev, had been part of a delegation of Soviet diplomats that had visited Australia just before we left for Moscow. There he had taken a shine to Lizzie, inviting her to swim with him at Bondi Beach, which she did. He was keen to see her again, though I'm not sure if he realised I was travelling with her and was her boyfriend. One of the two flash cars held Mr Afanasyev and Mr Grigorovich, and the other contained me, Lizzie and Mr Afanasyev's daughter, who spoke excellent English. We were whisked away for a half-hour drive to Mr Afanasyev's dacha, where we were given a full supper. Despite the intrigue, all I could think about was taking my poor exhausted body back to bed. It was after supper that Mr Grigorovich asked us what we would like to dance when we came back to Moscow to perform with the Bolshoi Ballet.

What? Perform with the Bolshoi? This was beyond anything we had imagined. I stared mutely at the green cabbage soup in front of me, which, when I finished it, revealed a portrait of Mr Afanasyev at the bottom. Fortunately, Lizzie had her wits about her. 'We're doing *Don Quixote* next year, so perhaps that?' she suggested, and Mr Grigorovich agreed. Just like that. At the end of the night, Mr Afanasyev presented Lizzie with an amazing full-sized replica of a samovar that Pushkin owned. I was given a small bronze replica of the Bolshoi Theatre – an accurate representation, I think, of where we stood in his affections.

This was one of the few nights we went home with full stomachs. We did, fortunately, become acquainted halfway through the competition with the staff at the Australian embassy, including John Denton and his (soon to be) wife, actor and comedian Jane Turner. Thanks to Maggie there had been a lunch at the embassy, with Ambassador Ted Pocock and his wife, Meg, organised for us during the competition, when Maggie could see we were getting thinner and thinner. It was sumptuous and I think Lizzie and I ate everything there was to eat in the kitchen. John and Jane also had us for dinner after the last round, which was another chance to up our calorie intake – they made us hamburgers and a rather delicious lemon cake. It had been a joy to be full again.

My bronze medal at the competition was awarded with 3000 rubles in prize money, which converted to about double that in Australian dollars – more money than I had ever had in my life. We spent one of our last days running around Moscow with John and Jane trying to buy keepsakes, but we didn't really make a dent in the winnings. After much wrangling, we ended up getting the leftover monies converted back to hard currency. That $6000 – an enormous sum of money in 1985 – was a delightful and unexpected consolation (along with an enduring friendship with the Pococks and the Dentons) from our Russian odyssey, and was enough for a deposit on a house.

Back in Australia, we were feted as a huge success story, with the 'couple on stage and off' theme still running strong. We did a lot of media: we performed part of the *Grand Tarantella* on Daryl Somers's hit television variety show *Hey, Hey, It's Saturday*, and we were on the cover of *Dance Australia*. It was a heady time. It felt almost like an out-of-body experience, with everyone suddenly interested in what you are doing and thinking. The first time Lizzie and I performed together in Melbourne after our return was as the Neapolitan couple in *Swan Lake* – people applauded us when we came on stage, which was crazy. No one ever applauds the Neapolitan couple.

Maina and Noel Pelly were delighted with our success. We told them that we had been invited back to dance with the Bolshoi, but this news was met with some scepticism from both. A couple of weeks later, their doubts were allayed when a telex (yes, this was the analog era) arrived with an invitation from the Bolshoi for us to perform with them in early 1986.

While my ballet career continued to soar, our relationship had come unstuck. Lizzie and I returned home to praise and constant attention, which was exhilarating and exhausting, and then picked up our lives in Falconer Street pretty much where we left off. But we had, domestically at least, fallen into a routine. The romance had tapered off as a consequence, and we were less physical than we had been in the early days.

Towards the end of the year we travelled to Adelaide to perform, and Lizzie dropped a bombshell. 'I think we should have some time out,' she said.

'What do you mean? Why?' I babbled, completely blindsided.

'I just think we need to have a break,' she replied.

In my inimitable style, I had not seen this coming, and I was utterly devastated. I was bewildered and distraught when we returned to Melbourne, which coincided with the Falconer Street house breaking up, as our other housemates changed careers or just moved on.

Lizzie suggested we buy a place together, as we were still uncertain about what to do with our award money. Even though this might seem like a profoundly daft move for a couple in the middle of ending their relationship, I agreed to it, nursing a secret hope that it might bring us back together. We bought a tiny two-bedroom worker's cottage quite close to our old Falconer Street rental home for $78,000. This time we had separate rooms, but we still lived together and shared digs very amicably. Our romantic partnership never reignited as I kept hoping it would. We retained a strong friendship and a great deal of affection for each other, but I kept trying to make it return to a romance and Lizzie, always so strong, kept telling me it was over. We lived together reasonably peaceably like this for about three years, during which time I managed to have a rather disastrous one-night stand (my first experience of such a thing) with another woman in the company who was stunning and lovely, which seemed an ideal revenge move to my poor addled brain. The thought of a relationship with her freaked me out – I was just not up for that level of heterosexuality, I think. Our night together was great for my ego and quelled some of my ongoing anxiety about my sexual prowess, but afterwards I told this beautiful woman that though she was amazing (and I meant it), a relationship wasn't quite right for me. Then, true to form, I ran away, in spirit at least. It was the last romantic attachment I had with anyone until Lizzie left the company.

All of this again made me question my sexuality – that knotty problem I could never seem to solve. When I was with Kelvin, I had wondered if I was truly gay, and then with Lizzie I had imagined a whole future that included a house, marriage and kids. All this swirled around in my mind after sleeping with just one other woman. Still in my head were the voices of those schoolyard bullies from all those years ago. I remained desperate to prove them wrong, desperate not to be gay.

The break-up with Lizzie really allowed me to get in touch with my inner diva. I regularly had dramatic crying fits, and if Lizzie went out for the evening, I'd drink a bottle of red wine and sit in our living room weeping and wondering who she was with. Fortunately, I had some good friends around me who dealt patiently with my theatrics. Our stage manager Margaret Bourke was one of those. She joined the company in 1985 and along with her velvety voice that played over the backstage address system, I really enjoyed her sense of humour and style. She had witnessed my rising career, but it was during my emotional split with Lizzie that we became very close friends. She was the one I poured my heart out to, repeatedly declaring my life as I knew it to be over, and I discovered that she was the most wonderful touring partner to share digs with. The other dear friend who got me through this time was Nerida O'Loughlin. Nerida had shared a flat with Lizzie when they were at the ballet school and later, having returned from London, moved into the Falconer Street house. Knowing my love for all things bridal, when the share house was breaking up, she bequeathed me her rather fetching powder-blue bridesmaid's dress, which I loved getting into during parties at that house and which still hangs in my closet at home. She was a fabulous ally during this sad time, and our friendship grew to be an unshakable bond. Along with Margaret, Nerida became one of my trusted confidants.

⁓

While all of this was going on, our 1986 return trip to the Bolshoi was fast approaching. Though Lizzie and I were not together, our public persona was very much connected, and so it was sort of business as usual at work and on tour. In my fantasy world, being connected with Lizzie professionally fed my belief that we would one day get back together. For that reason, and because our friendship had survived our break-up, it was a happy time.

We were performing *Don Quixote* – probably one of my favourite ballets of all time. The Russians, during those communist times, traditionally first sent guest artists somewhere else in the Soviet Union to perform before dancing in the capital, to make sure their standard hadn't dropped and the exacting Moscow audiences wouldn't be disappointed. If it had, there would suddenly be a scheduling 'cancellation' and the invitation would unfortunately be revoked. We were taken to Vilnius in Lithuania, where we did a couple of performances of *Don Quixote*. Interestingly, this was the birthplace of Janina Cunova, with whom I had enjoyed working at The Australian Ballet School. Although it had been decades since she had been to her birthplace, she was still remembered very fondly and we were feted for being her students. Vilnius was stunning and we seemed to pass the test, so from there we travelled to Moscow, where this time we were invited to stay at the Australian embassy.

When guest artists perform a classic ballet like *Don Quixote* with an established company, they often dance a combination of two quite different versions. Usually there is some kind of compromise – the company will keep in the parts that the guests are especially wedded to and don't affect the overall production, but they will have the guests learn what the company does for the rest, particularly the big scenes with large numbers of dancers. Having performed with a different company in Vilnius, we had yet another production to meld with at the Bolshoi Ballet, though we had a pretty good idea of what we needed to learn and what we could do in our own way. Obviously, the stakes were much higher this time, as we were dancing *Don Quixote* with the company that had premiered this ballet and performed it continuously since 1869.

Our big Moscow performance was on 23 April (I still have the poster for it on my bedroom wall). It went very well, except for one of those episodes that makes for a great dinner party story later in life. The first and second acts went smoothly. I enjoyed my trio in Act I with the two girlfriends, and Lizzie and I managed to get through all of the different mime scenes without confusing any of the cast. We had a few little sections to learn in the third act, which we mastered without mishap, and then there was only the grand pas de deux left to complete. The duet went well and we managed all the tricky sections of partnering, which always made me feel confident going into the solos. I knew there was a bridesmaid solo before I entered to dance my solo, but I was unaware that there was another bridesmaid who danced before the coda. I entered after Lizzie's solo to prepare for the coda, only to be greeted by the bemused faces of the dancers sitting around me who started saying 'nyet, nyet'. Just then I saw a flash of yellow tutu entering the stage – the second bridesmaid was bearing down, at which point I gallantly gestured to her as I left the stage. After she had finished, feeling confident it was now my turn, I entered again and the audience erupted in supportive applause, gently mocking my mistake. I launched into the coda with added verve. As I was heading into the *manège*, a circle step of *jeté élancé* (which I had perfected on the oval at Debney Park all those years ago), I managed to stub my toe and, after the first flying *fouetté* combination, ended up on the floor. Having gathered immense forward motion, I managed to continue into a commando roll and be back on my feet and into the next set of *jetés* to complete the rest of the circular step. I couldn't believe I had just fallen on the Bolshoi stage! As is always the case in performance, the audience loved a good fall, and I managed to redeem myself with a flawless grand pirouette. After our finale, we enjoyed the sort of ovation that is rarely received outside of Russia. It was certainly a night to remember.

Afterwards, the ambassador Ted Pocock and his wife, Meg, organised a huge party for us. At the party we overheard two rather posh, English-sounding women – expat Australians, I think – talking to each other: 'Well, we thought we were going to see the Bolshoi and then all of a sudden these two Or-stralians come out, but they were very good.' They repeated this story to pretty much everyone in the room. Lizzie and I laughed and laughed about it.

After the party, we went to the Bolshoi's dormitories, as several dancers from the competition had come to Moscow to see our show. We snuck in a bottle of brandy from the Australian embassy and partied with the other dancers for most of the night. The evening ended with me, very glamorously, falling asleep on my knees hugging the toilet, as I thought I was going to be sick. We crept back to the embassy early the next day before catching our plane home – needless to say, we slept a lot on the flight. The Russians we encountered throughout our visit assumed we were married because our identities were so interlinked, and we didn't bother to correct them.

Our love affair with Russia – and theirs with us – lasted for a long time. Lizzie and I were invited back to Moscow in 1987, when we danced some gala concerts at the Tchaikovsky Hall with Evelyn Hart and André Lewis from Canada's Royal Winnipeg Ballet, as well as some dancers from around the Soviet Union. Once again we danced the *Grand Tarantella*, as we did every time we visited Russia – it was our passport to being asked back. Nina Ananiashvili and Andris Liepa, both principals with the Bolshoi, were also there. One of the most memorable evenings of this visit was meeting Andris's father, the famous Bolshoi dancer Māris Liepa, who told us how much he enjoyed the *Grand Tarantella*. While we were there we also danced in a performance of *Giselle* at the Kremlin Palace Theatre, where the stage was huge, the biggest I've ever seen. We were to dance the Peasant pas de deux, which in the Australian version is a centrepiece pas de deux in the first act. It was the dance that had started my career, back with my first performance for The Dancers Company. When we arrived at the Kremlin, we were more than a little surprised to discover a group of peasants with tambourines taking part in the performance. Given that tambourines would be more at home in an Italian mardi gras than a German harvest festival, it created a more spirited take on this dance than we were used to. For us, this was a rather unexpected version of the classic. Giselle and Albrecht were danced by Nina Semizorova and Aleksandr Bogatyrev, current stars of the Bolshoi. Later, Aleksandr came to Melbourne with another Russian ballerina, Galina Shlyapina, to dance *Swan Lake* with The Australian Ballet. We did our best to cover the enormous Kremlin Palace stage during the Peasant pas de deux but it was a big ask, even with the tambourine chorus. Adding to our great excitement was that Nina was coached by the legendary Galina Ulanova, who came to Australia the following year to coach Lisa Pavane and Greg Horsman in *Giselle*.

Our fourth and final trip to the Soviet Union as a dancing couple was in March and April of 1988. This time, our out-of-town 'audition' performance was in Tbilisi, Georgia, where we performed *Don Quixote* and again seemed to pass muster. Afterwards, we made our way to Moscow to perform a gala concert, which was rather grandly called the All-Stars of Ballet. Naturally, we danced the *Grand Tarantella*, but this time we had a new ballet in our arsenal as well: Petal Miller, who was Maina's assistant on the ballet staff and also choreographed a number of works for the company, created a piece for us to Glenn Miller's music called *Miller Swing*. It was wonderful to have a less physically demanding but extremely fun piece to dance – it was very different from any of the other pas de deux we had performed. We also danced the so-called Fanny Elssler pas de deux from *La Fille mal gardée* (the one we had performed in the competition), after which we caught the train to Leningrad, where we were to be the first Australian guest artists to perform with the Kirov Ballet. We were in Leningrad for just under two days and it was all a bit of a whirlwind. At the fifteen-minute call, there was an announcement to the company that, roughly interpreted, went something like this: 'This is your fifteen-minute call. Tonight we have two Australian guest artists with us who have been here a very short time and have not seen our production. They may dance some different choreography from ours, so if they start dancing towards you, please get out of their way.'

After the effusiveness of the Bolshoi, dancing with the Kirov was quite a culture shock.

The dancers were a little frosty towards us because we were seen as 'Moscow people', having been in the competition there. The visit was so quick, however, that we really didn't have the chance to get to know them, nor they us. And there was the language barrier. During the performance, I was in the wings watching Lizzie perform the Dryad scene, when a Russian dancer in Kitri costume grabbed me by the hand and led me onto the stage. It seemed they had forgotten to tell me that I was to make an entrance during that scene, and as the dancer didn't speak any English and my Russian was rudimentary to say the least, I was forced to ad-lib. We must have performed well enough, though, because at the end of the show, the whole company stayed on stage after the curtain calls and gave us a wonderfully warm ovation. It's a shame we didn't have more time to spend in Leningrad, but we needed to catch a train straight after the show to Tallinn in Estonia, where we did two more performances of *Don Quixote* with the Estonian National Ballet.

It was an amazing time to have this rich experience abroad. I never dreamed that I would have all these opportunities that flowed from Maina sending us to the ballet competition in Moscow. It fundamentally changed me as a dancer and was the catalyst for how I developed over the rest of my career. Not only did I dance with some of the greatest dancers of my generation at the competition, but I had the chance to return three more times to dance with two of the most important companies in the ballet world. It was also a time of great upheaval for the Soviet Union. Gorbachev was opening up the country, something that had been unimaginable only years before. Each trip, we saw the beginning and growth of solo enterprise, which led ultimately to the fall of communism. It was also fascinating to experience firsthand that despite the dogma we had been fed in the West since childhood regarding the Russian people, they were so wonderful, cultured and friendly. The system was deeply flawed, yes, but the kindness and friendship we experienced over these visits was unparalleled. Friendships were forged quickly, and bonds created were upheld for many years. I think of this time with incredible fondness and gratitude.

Back home, it seemed to us that Maina was not as thrilled about these Russian invitations as we might have hoped. She may have thought it would be better to spread the trips around to other dancers, but it was Lizzie and me that they kept inviting back. I had been promoted rapidly since joining the company, and by 1987 I was a senior artist, but I was dancing quite a few principal roles. There was, though, still the 'I don't see you as a prince' conversation ringing in my ears, and I wondered if I would ever be made a principal.

When we were in Sydney that year performing Anne Woolliams's *Swan Lake*, a small electrical fire at the Opera House meant that a matinee we were scheduled to perform had to be cancelled. While this drama was happening, all the Opera House occupants including the dancers were ushered out to the Opera House forecourt to wait until the fire brigade told us we could return. We'd just completed a class ahead of the scheduled matinee, and half the company was in stage make-up as we chattered away. Whenever there was a big announcement within the company – usually a dancer being made a principal – someone would bang on the 'virtual' tom-toms and the news would be spread. On this strange day, the tom-toms were in overdrive as we learnt that Fiona Tonkin had been made principal. Everyone was chatting and celebrating – it was a big deal. Then it went around almost as quickly that Greg Horsman had also been promoted to principal. And finally, one more announcement: there was one more new principal, and it was ... Steve Heathcote. But not me. I was not on the list.

When we were allowed back into the Opera House, I was informed that Maina wanted to see me. 'Ooooh,' people around me started saying, 'you're next, you're going to be promoted, too!'

I went around to Maina's office, my heart pounding in my chest, and knocked on her door. When I sat down, she said: 'You've probably heard that I've promoted Fiona, Greg and Steve, and I just wanted you to know that I'm not promoting you.'

It was a bit of a blow, I can't deny, but I was determined not to show it. 'Oh, that's fine,' I said. Maina continued: 'I wanted you to know, because obviously you've been promoted through the ranks together; I feel that they're ready at the moment, but there's still some things for you to develop. It's not that I don't see you as being a principal, but it's just not now.'

In hindsight, I can see that Maina meant well in explaining her reasoning; she was trying to stop me from feeling disenchanted or pissed off and perhaps even leaving. But with all the attention around the promotions – and everyone knowing that I *wasn't* promoted – it was hard not to feel bitterly disappointed, even with my generally optimistic nature.

Initially, I resorted to my usual 'I'll show you!' response in the months after being overlooked. I kept doing more and more and working harder and harder, but still nothing changed, and I began to think that I had perhaps hit the limit of my potential within The Australian Ballet. Could it be that there was a natural ceiling for all dancers and mine was senior artist? I hoped not, and while I was trying to be a realist, I felt I had more to give. It certainly was not a happy thought.

Lizzie and I continued to get on fabulously as friends – but we were never again lovers. With me still lovelorn and hoping (wildly against the evidence) that this might change, sharing a house became a bit uncomfortable. This was especially so when Lizzie started dating Paul de Masson. I really liked Paul – I admired him as an artist and we were quite friendly. But the thought of another man – especially another male dancer – sharing a bed with Lizzie was more than I could bear. I consoled myself by thinking that I was a better dancer than he was (even though he had been a principal for some years). Classic break-up stuff.

One morning, after Paul had stayed the night, I got in my car and drove to the Edinburgh Gardens, which were not even a block away. I parked and sat crying, feeling sorry for myself. My friend Robyn Fynmore, whom I had known and admired since my first year at the school when she was dancing as a guest artist with The Dancers Company, tapped on the window and asked me what I was doing. She was living with her sister nearby and was out for a morning walk before she found me. 'I had to get out of the house!' I wailed. I was a little dramatic. We ended up having coffee and she helped pull me together – another member of 'team Daisy' whom I have been so lucky to have as a friend.

Meanwhile, there continued to be a fair bit of media interest in me and Lizzie, and while we never pushed the idea that we were a couple, we didn't discourage it, either. This eventually landed me in hot water with my mum, when Lizzie and I were interviewed for an arts show on the ABC. At the end of the program, the presenter said something along the lines of: 'And not only are they a couple on stage, but it wouldn't be surprising if they were soon to announce their engagement.' *Oh my god*, I thought as I watched it afterwards, and sure enough, three hours later after it had screened in Perth, the phone rang. It was my mother and she was not happy – in fact, her voice was uncharacteristically cold. 'I thought you'd at least let your parents know you were getting engaged first before announcing it on national television,' she said through clenched teeth. Ironically, Lizzie and I had hit a really rough patch at the time and were barely speaking. I assured my mum that I was as shocked as she was, and nothing of the sort was going to happen.

Looking back, I think my mum and dad, quite understandably, found my relationship with Lizzie confusing, and suspected I wasn't being entirely honest with them. I mean, we were a couple, then not a couple, then we were buying a house and living together – what on earth was going on? I can see how strange it must have seemed to them.

And slowly it was dawning on me, too, that buying a house together had been a big mistake. By the final months of 1988, we had been living together platonically for almost three years, and it seemed that Lizzie and Paul's relationship was becoming serious. When we bought the house together, we had agreed that if one of us wanted to sell, the other had to sell, too, unless one could buy the other out. I told Lizzie that I wanted to sell and that I didn't want to live with her anymore – she should go and live with Paul. She didn't want to sell, but I insisted.

With my professional and personal lives in a bit of a funk, Maina may have picked up on my restlessness, as she made plans to send me on exchange to The National Ballet of Canada. It seemed like the perfect out clause and The National Ballet was the ideal choice, as I had felt so at home there all those years ago when I had visited the company on my 'Christmas kids' scholarship in my first year at The Australian Ballet. With the promise of the trip on the horizon, I began to consider the idea that once I was in Canada, I might decide not to return to Australia as there didn't seem to be many prospects at home. I would sell the house, pack up all my stuff, and see what North America had to offer me. I shared these plans, and my lack of hope in ever being made principal, with Noel Pelly, who I suspect may have let Maina know I was thinking that way.

Before heading off to Canada, I went to my usual end-of-year interview with Maina, planning to ask her for a year's leave of absence following on from my upcoming exchange (a little insurance policy in case my plan to stay in North America didn't work out). Just as I was gearing up to ask, Maina said: 'Oh, and I'd like you to go to Canada as a principal.' She followed this up with some generous praise for my performances in the past year, which had included the supremely princely role of Albrecht in *Giselle*. Finally, my day had come – there was no ceiling!

Our house was sold just before Christmas. I stayed with Margaret Bourke, my touring buddy and dear friend, in St Kilda for a short while, and then I jetted off to Canada for a three-month stint as a guest artist. I did so in the knowledge that the dream I had so lovingly nursed since I was a little boy watching Nureyev on television had come true at last: I was a principal artist with The Australian Ballet. Princes could be short and have big noses after all.

CHAPTER 6

Principal syndrome

There's a malaise I have seen many times in my career, both as a dancer and an artistic director – I call it 'principal syndrome'. It goes like this: an ambitious and hard-working young person strives so hard to achieve the rank of principal, but when they get there (after a honeymoon period of about six months or so), they wonder, *Now what?* And not being able to clearly answer that question can lead them to feel a little lost, having nothing to push against. Of course, there is always more to strive for – a role, an international tour, being able to perform a particular step with ease or work with a particular choreographer – but sometimes dancers can feel a bit rudderless without the clear ranks of the company to climb.

The principal syndrome manifested itself for me through injury – not just one, but several in a row. Until I reached principal, I had been blessed in terms of injury, having suffered very few in my career and none of them being particularly bad. (Those four or five years of nonstop anti-inflammatory consumption were not exactly medical best practice, but they did keep me on the stage.) I jetted off to Toronto on an amazing high, having been promoted and looking forward to returning after my wonderful exchange in Canada. It also gave me some much-needed time out from the personal dramas with Lizzie and the stress of selling the house. It allowed me to reset and do what I did best: devote myself to my work.

They were three precious months away from Australia and the company. I got to dance with a whole new group of people and perform roles I was familiar with – such as Benvolio and Mercutio in John Cranko's *Romeo and Juliet* and the principal boy in Harald Lander's *Études* – as well as parts I had not been cast in at home, such as the Sanguinic pas de deux in George Balanchine's *The Four Temperaments*. I danced on the stage with an icon of Canadian ballet, Karen Kain, and performed with Italian prima ballerina Alessandra Ferri, who was a guest artist and huge international star at that time. I also met so many people who remained friends through the rest of my career. It was a nourishing experience that came at the perfect time for me to grow and mature.

When I returned to Australia in March 1989, I immediately went into rehearsals for *La Fille mal gardée*, which I was to dance with Fiona Tonkin. We were also chosen as the lead dancers for the ABC broadcast of the ballet, which was an added thrill. We completed the taping first, which went well, then we continued with the season. It was in one particularly memorable show that my injury-free run began to unravel. Fiona and I were doing the so-called door pas de deux in the third act, which is when Colas (my character) stands on a bunch of hay bales behind a closed door and, through an opening in the top of the door, dances with Lise (Colas's 'love interest' in the ballet). The hay bales shifted beneath me at one point, and as I was hunched forward in an awkward position, I felt a tug in my lower back. As we finished the performance, I came off stage thinking something was not right. I was stiff and there was some pain, but in the spirit of the times, I kept going, hoping it would simply mend itself overnight.

It did not. The next morning I was even more stiff and sore, but with a little treatment it subsided and I finished the season. Fortuitously, this led into our midyear break, which I thought would be the perfect time for my back to heal properly. But it got worse and worse, and when I returned to work to begin rehearsals for *Onegin*, in which I was dancing Lensky, my back was still causing me considerable pain. One day, as I was doing warm-up exercises at the barre, I felt almost completely numb down my legs, apart from a strange buzzing in my toe. I went to see a physiotherapist and then a doctor who immediately banned me from dancing for a week, but the symptoms only got worse. Scans revealed that I had a herniated disc in my back – an L5-S1 bulge. I took another two weeks off and had a jab of cortisone, but neither did anything to improve it. Suddenly, I was forced off dancing for two months, then three. Then I started to develop 'foot drop', where the nerve is so damaged that you can't lift up the front of your foot.

It was getting very serious indeed, and I was worried. This was not eased at all when the company's consulting orthopaedic doctor and head of the medical team, Ken Crichton, took me to see a neurologist called David Vivian. In the taxi on the way to see the specialist, Ken asked: 'So have you ever thought of doing anything other than dancing?' The question, meant kindly, was nonetheless like a knife in my chest. I was twenty-six years old and the answer, of course, was no. It had always been ballet, and nothing but ballet, since the time I was prancing around the family living room in front of the turned-off television. 'No, Ken,' I replied. 'I don't have a plan B.'

During the consultation, the doctors talked about the possibility of a percutaneous discectomy, a procedure that involves a fine instrument removing the part of the herniated disc that is pressing on the nerve. But such a procedure carried risks, among them the likelihood of narrowing my range of movement. This is particularly difficult for a ballet dancer as L5-S1 is very important for achieving and maintaining a good line in arabesque, and arabesque for us is like kicking for a footballer – there's really no performing without it.

I knew my injury was serious, and I knew of other dancers whose careers had been ended by the same one. But I was lucky: I still had a range of movement, especially bending forward, which is unusual with a herniated disc, and David Vivian saw the potential for a non-surgical solution. He ordered me to have complete bed rest for a week, then I could get to work on a slow recovery. Determined this would not end my career, I did exactly as he said, staying with Robyn Fynmore (the good friend who had come to my rescue when I was a blubbering mess in the car at Edinburgh Gardens) at her dad's house, which she was looking after while he was away. I literally didn't get out of bed for a week except to go to the toilet. Robyn was incredible: she brought in breakfast for me every morning and left me lunch, then cooked dinner for us at night. I felt like an invalid and a bit of a burden, but it worked: all of a sudden, after that week, the neural symptoms started to subside and, to my immense relief, the horrible buzzing in my toe started to go away.

The recovery was slow but steady – in fact, I could almost trace its journey up my leg to my back. I felt like I could perceive the nerves slowly reconnecting from my toe, and things returning to normal. Every week I saw physiotherapist Mike Ralston, who'd ask me to do a straight leg raise to assess how much movement I had. In the first week I could move less than 10 centimetres, but eventually I could lift it to 90 degrees without any nerve pain, which meant I was ready for gentle class work with our ballet mistress Noelle Shader, who had become an expert in dancer rehabilitation. Such relief! Mike also suggested I do some hydrotherapy to ease back into the physical workload. I took myself off to a nearby pool to complete some laps walking through the water, as I had been instructed, and found I was completely exhausted – my performance fitness had totally crashed during the time off.

In the course of my rehabilitation, I had to go and see Maina for my annual review and to discuss the program for the following year. I was wearing a huge, boned corset type of contraption to keep my back in alignment as I sat myself down – gingerly – to discuss my contract. 'We're doing *Spartacus*,' enthused Maina, 'and I thought you could dance Spartacus!' I was enthusiastic in my response, because I genuinely wanted to dance such a brilliant role for a male lead, but in my head I was panicking. *Oh my god*, I thought, *I've just been exhausted by walking across a pool in water up to my chest. Dance Spartacus? I don't think so.*

But it was months away, so I reasoned I still had some time. I started doing Pilates to strengthen my core, making me realise my abdominal muscles were much weaker than I had imagined. I also travelled to Sydney to see osteopath Ross Partington at the recommendation of choreographer Graeme Murphy and his partner, Janet Vernon, and the combination of treatments proved a winner, because by the end of the year I was back in class with the company – and hoping like hell my back would hold up.

The company had moved into our wonderful, luxurious new headquarters at Southbank the year before, in 1988 – such a change from Flemington – and soon after we had our very own Pilates studio run by Andrew Baxter. This meant my rehab could now be managed entirely in-house by people who specialised in treating dancers, which was really helpful to me in returning to full strength. As planned, we started the new year 1990 with *Spartacus*, but my back was not yet up to dancing in it, so I waited until the next production, which was *Onegin* – ironically, the ballet I had been rehearsing when I finally gave in to my injured back.

I was terrified of reinjuring my back, and I had a few nerve-racking episodes, but by this stage I had gained enough knowledge through my treatment and rehab to know that if it was just localised pain, it was probably muscular and that was okay. If it was nerve pain, I knew to pull back. It was a conservative return to full duties, but it actually set me up for the remaining eleven years of my career by making me more aware of my body and protective of it. By the time we toured to New York in the middle of the year, I was able to dance Albrecht in *Giselle* without any problems.

A few months later, Liz (as I had begun calling her) announced she was leaving the company. Having had some distance placed between us by my Canada exchange and my injury, we were again friends and able to enjoy each other's company. Liz was leaving as a senior artist to spread her wings, and I started to feel the slightest niggle of restlessness myself. Should I, too, leave the company and broaden my horizons, perhaps try to join a company overseas?

During the Christmas break in 1990 and early 1991, I headed to Europe to try to answer that question, visiting several European companies, taking classes and talking with people. It was a valuable thing to do, because it made me recognise that The Australian Ballet was doing work every bit as interesting as these companies.

I realised that if I went overseas, it would be like starting over and proving myself again – which would likely mean an extended period of dancing much smaller, less challenging roles. I returned to work in Melbourne in 1991 much happier and more contented for the experience, knowing that The Australian Ballet was absolutely the right company for me.

Just before this trip, I managed to break my rule of never again dating a dancer within the company. With my heart mended and my career back on track after injury, my confidence was restored. I was spending a lot of time with Jayne Beddoe, a wonderful dancer whose zest for life and outgoing personality I found completely intoxicating. We loved hanging out together. When the company was in Adelaide, I shared a rather lovely, homely apartment with Margaret Bourke, my regular touring flatmate. One Sunday, Jayne and I were meeting up to go and do something, but it instead turned into a very passionate afternoon in my living room and the start of an exciting relationship. It was wonderful to once again be in a relationship – and to have the girlfriend I still thought would make me 'normal' – and I relished what felt like a fun summer romance.

But then the European trip of self-discovery came along. While I was in Europe, I visited some old friends, including Liz in London, who had met a lovely Swede who later became her husband. My travels helped me to realise not only that The Australian Ballet was the only place for me, but also that I had to face up to how much I valued being on my own. My relationship with Jayne had only been for a few months and I had enjoyed every minute of it, but I knew it was not going to last. If I had been willing and able at this stage to be truly honest with myself, I would have known that I would never be able to give Jayne – or any woman – what she wanted. That realisation, conscious at least, was still a few years away. Instead, I returned home to Melbourne to end the fledgling relationship. I felt terrible about it because I really did love Jayne and our time together, but being a couple was just not right for me at that time. Thankfully, we have always remained great friends.

Once again, the question of whether I preferred to be sleeping with men was nipping at my heels. I liked being with women and wanted to be with them, but I also didn't want to be someone who settled down with a woman and had children, while sneaking off to be with men on the side. To mask my internal confusion, I maintained my determination to be a paradox at work. I think one of the peripheral reasons I was reluctant to explore my sexuality – apart from not wanting to be what the bullies had always labelled me – was that I worried there would be some kind of authenticity problem in playing straight male leads on stage. Could I be a convincing male lead, tormented in love as so many of ballet's male leads are, if the audience knew I was going home to a male partner? I realise now how ridiculously naive that sounds. I've seen countless gay men portray straight men convincingly, and vice versa (it's called acting, David). I also know that when you are on stage and deeply immersed in a ballet, in a sense you do fall in love at that moment, so it's hardly a reach at all. But somehow, in my confused head, it was an issue, and one that might jeopardise my career.

I had had a scare, too. A couple of years earlier, Jack and Shirley Toohey – Liz's parents – had been visiting for the Melbourne Cup at a time when I was struggling with an ongoing illness. Lizzie and

I were no longer a couple, but I was still very fond of her mum and dad, and they were staying with us. Jack was a GP, and I told him I had been feeling very sick, with night sweats and nausea. 'Oh mate,' he said, 'it sounds like glandular fever. You'd better get yourself to a doctor.' I did just that, and the first thing the doctor asked me was what I did for a living. 'I'm a ballet dancer,' I said. He asked for my symptoms, to which I replied night sweats and fatigue. He asked if I'd lost weight recently and I said I had, but that I'd been working very hard.

'Well,' he said, 'you have all the signs of HIV. Have you had any exposure?'

I could barely breathe. At that time, an HIV diagnosis was akin to a death sentence, with treatment nowhere near as effective as it is today. Sometime earlier, Kelvin had shared with Liz and me that he had been diagnosed with HIV. 'Yee-es,' I stammered, and the doctor sent me off immediately for a test.

I returned to the Ballet Centre, ashen, and told Liz. 'No, it couldn't be possible,' she reassured me. But it was possible. It took an agonising week for the results to come back, during which everything else fell away as I wondered if I could be dying. Finally, after returning to the doctor for the results, he was pleased to tell me that the test was negative, and I nearly collapsed with relief. Further tests then revealed that, just as Jack had suspected, I had glandular fever, from which I was lucky enough to make a swift recovery.

For Kelvin, though, the news was grim – the HIV had turned into an AIDS-related illness, and he was dying. He had been 'outed' with his illness unwillingly, because he was a well-known figure who had become even better known during the dancers' strike. He was also very private, but just as he had during the strike, he put that to one side to become a spokesperson on living with the disease. He agreed to an interview with the ABC about his illness, and it had been quite a dramatic event within the Ballet Centre.

Kelvin was teaching at the ballet school and we saw each other occasionally, but with touring and everything else, we had not spent as much time together as we did in my earlier days with the company. If we saw each other in the corridors, we'd always stop and chat – sometimes I could see he was struggling with his health; other times he seemed to be okay. He was actually very sick while he was teaching, but he remained stoic and strong. He knew the illness was going to take his life, and too soon, but he was determined to make the most of whatever time he had left.

Once he stopped working, he deteriorated quickly. In early 1992, the company was preparing to head to London for its thirtieth anniversary celebrations. We heard that Kelvin was very sick, and so before we left on tour, Liz – who had left the company but was in Melbourne – and I went to see him, knowing that it might be for the last time. He had been in hospital but had returned home for palliative care. We walked into his house and there he was, that familiar, kind face now pale and gaunt. I remember looking at him and marvelling at the peace and acceptance he expressed. He was surrounded by people who were caring for him, including his partner, Stuart, and it was a warm, caring and beautiful experience to be with him that day.

Still, I couldn't help but feel a little guilty. Could I have done more for this wonderful man, who had been so instrumental in my career and personal life? It left me unsettled and worried.

It was a time of emotional extremes because soon after visiting Kelvin we left for London, which was an absolute privilege and a career highlight. The company travelled first to Italy, where we performed outdoors at the Nervi Festival, before heading to London for a season of *Coppélia* at the Coliseum theatre in the West End. There was some anxiety that a strike in France would prevent the sets and costumes from arriving in time, but mercifully they got there and the show could go on. Miranda Coney – a fellow principal whom I had known back in my Perth City Ballet days when we were children – and I were to dance the leads in *Coppélia* for the Royal Gala in front of Princess Diana. It was incredibly stressful. The dress rehearsal had been a disaster, I think in part because I couldn't stop thinking about performing for the princess, a known ballet lover and one of the most stylish and beautiful people in the world. I was terrified of putting in a bad performance.

The next morning, with the show that night, I woke up vowing I was not going to be nervous but excited. I came to the theatre determined to enjoy myself hugely – it was the most effective way of dealing with my own expectations as well as those of the other dancers and the company's management. *If I can get through Moscow*, I told myself, and not for the first time, *I can get through this*. A security sweep through the theatre before the performance made us even more aware of our royal guest.

From the minute the curtain went up, it was one of the few shows in which I can honestly say I don't think I put a foot wrong. The entire company was on fire that night. Everything just seemed to happen effortlessly; I even started taking a few risks with steps – and they paid off. Miranda was so much fun to dance with and I felt like we had a real connection – the whole performance was a joy and one of the best nights of my life.

At the end of the show, after the curtain calls, Princess Diana came up on stage and we were presented to her. She was absolutely radiant – a vision in a long peach and cream gown to her ankles, and so much more beautiful than even the best photographs of her. I was completely overwhelmed, and when she came to talk to us I was a tongue-tied mess. I can't even remember what I said, but I doubt any of it made sense. I went back to the dressing room thinking I had just blown my special moment with the most famous woman on the planet. I knew some of us were being invited to a function after the performance, so I made a pact with myself that if I saw her there I wouldn't gibber like an idiot; I would talk to her like a normal human being.

After we changed back into our civilian clothes, we were taken to St James's Palace, where a few of us had been chosen to mix with British high society – including royalty. Miranda, Maina and I were there along with some other dancers from The Australian Ballet, including Colin Peasley (who had performed as Dr Coppelius that night), Jayne Beddoe, Vicki Attard and Lisa Bolte. We all thought we would be at a table with Princess Diana, but it turned out she was on another table, with a seat next to her that was occupied by a revolving circuit of people throughout the night. I was on a table with some charming people from Chanel and was having a great time. Just before dessert, Lady Potter, one of our generous patrons and the host for the evening, came and asked me if I would like to have five minutes with the guest of honour. I was sitting next to the princess before Lady Potter could finish her sentence. As luck would have it, this was precisely as dessert was being served, which, according to protocol, meant I couldn't be moved along until the plates had been cleared.

We had about fifteen minutes together while she grappled with her peach sorbet (that was actually served in the shape of a peach) – it was so frozen she asked for a knife to cut into it, and we both spent the next few minutes trying to hack into it, in vain. The princess immediately made me feel at ease, like we were old friends. We talked about her dancing, her favourite ballet (*Romeo and Juliet*), Chanel shoes and our performance, which thankfully she liked. It was all a little surreal. Who would have thought that a daggy little kid showing off on a septic tank in suburban Perth would one day have dessert with a princess?

The rest of the company's performances in London ran smoothly. But while we were there, Maina told us one day that Kelvin had died. He was just forty-five. I knew this news was coming, but it was still a shock, a huge blow. I didn't actually know many people who had died, at least not anyone I had known as well as Kelvin, apart from my grandmother. I wasn't very good at grieving, or facing unpleasant emotions, so I took the news and locked it away, telling myself I would open it up and take a look at it later, when I was ready.

When I did finally unlock that grief and think about him, several weeks later, I wondered again about the nagging guilt I felt in relation to Kelvin. I think I felt a little guilty that I couldn't be the person he had wanted me to be, at least not at that time in my life, or maybe ever. He was never angry or bitter about it, and we maintained our great friendship until the end. He gave me the space to make the mistakes I needed to make and figure myself out: he never said, 'Come on, be honest with yourself; you like men and we should be together.' He stood back and let me stumble down that road on my own.

He had also meant so much to me as a dancing idol, mentor and teacher – we had danced together right up until 1988. He was someone I always wanted to impress, and he was always brutally honest. 'That wasn't a great show,' he'd say, or 'Your legs look tired' or 'You really should work on this.' But it was always constructive and never mean, and he always asked me how I was – and genuinely wanted to hear the answer.

There was a time when Kelvin had wanted to be the artistic director of the company. I think he would have been brilliant at it. When I became artistic director, it occurred to me that Kelvin would have been one of the people whose opinion I would have wanted very much, especially early on. That said, it might have been utterly confusing because I cared so much what he thought. I owe a lot to him, and he will always be a giant figure of Australian ballet.

I continued to dance relatively injury-free. My back flared up a couple of times, but I was usually able to get it to settle reasonably quickly. Then in 1993, while rehearsing *Giselle* with Vicki Attard, I sprained my ankle. I was bitterly disappointed that I'd injured myself, as I'd been looking forward to dancing Albrecht again. At the time we were also rehearsing a contemporary program by renowned Czech choreographer Jiří Kylián that I was featured in, so I wanted to recover as soon as possible. It was only a mild sprain and did indeed seem to mend quickly. I went to see the company's physiotherapist, Sarah Way, who had navigated the path through my back injury with me and had then handed me into the care of her husband, Mike Ralston, when their first son, James, was due. I enthused to Sarah, 'Look, I can do this! It's all good now,' as I jumped up and down on my injured ankle.

'That's great, but just be careful,' she cautioned.

I went back into *Giselle* rehearsals that afternoon and, such was my confidence, thought I would test the ankle with a few cabrioles, where you extend a leg in front (or behind) in a jump and pick up the other leg to meet it. And then came the sound no dancer wants to hear: *craaack*.

We were due to travel to Japan and China in twelve weeks, where I was to dance the Prince in *The Sleeping Beauty*. I was devastated. Scans revealed a clean break of my fifth metatarsal, one of the long bones in the foot. My premature confidence that the sprain had healed led me to push too hard too soon (just as Sarah had warned against). Now the loss of strength and condition had led to the break. The doctors told me that if I was really sensible – that is, the opposite of what I had been with the sprained ankle – I might be able to get back in time to tour. This meant the next six weeks on crutches, with me unable to bear weight on my injured foot. Again, the rehabilitation seemed very slow. I managed to recover enough to go on tour, though with significantly reduced duties – I made it back in time for one performance of *Beauty* in Tokyo but for most of the tour danced *Forgotten Land* in a role that was mostly partnering and didn't require much jumping.

I was turning thirty at the end of the tour in Tokyo, and I was determined to be back dancing fully by my big day in November. I managed that, which thrilled me, and shortly after that I travelled to Birmingham on exchange with the Birmingham Royal Ballet. My foot was holding up but was still not back to normal, so I used the excuse of jet lag to reduce my workload for a few days in the hope it would improve and to avoid reinjuring the freshly healed fracture. Eventually I ended up confessing to the lovely ballet master, Desmond Kelly, that I had just returned from injury.

'Why didn't you tell me?' he asked, very reasonably.

'Oh, well, I didn't want to be *that* dancer,' was my lame reply. But, of course, I was that other kind of dancer – the one who keeps trying to pretend he's in good shape when he's not. With Desmond now fully aware of the situation, the rest of the exchange went extremely well.

My run of injury was unfortunately not yet over, and my return to Melbourne brought a new problem. I had had bone spurs around both ankles for a few years, and by this stage one of them in particular was bothering me – they were like little teeth, biting into each other every time I sank into plié. This meant my plié was getting more and more shallow, and something had to be done. I've always suspected that the bone spurs might have led to my back injury, too, because it meant I wasn't landing properly out of jumps, putting huge strain on my lower back.

I went to see surgeon Kim Slater, who looked at the scans of both ankles and told me that as they were as bad as each other, he might as well operate on both at once. I would be unable to perform for twelve weeks, so I completed the Sydney season, then had the surgery and spent a week in Sydney recovering. Within a week, I was back in the studio to begin another rehab. The surgery was so successful that by the end of the twelve weeks, I returned to dancing and was able to be part of the creation of the hugely demanding ballet *Divergence* with Stanton Welch. Thanks to the brilliant work of my surgeon, my ankles never bothered me again.

By the start of the 1995 season, I was raring to go. *Finally*, I thought, *I'm free of injury and in the prime of my career* – I was turning thirty-two but determined to show all those talented young blokes rising up through the ranks just what I could do. I was getting to that stage in my profession – and by now I had had a few years of interruptions due to injury – when it was hard to not occasionally look over my shoulder. And what I saw was an awful lot of talent approaching rather rapidly behind me.

We were rehearsing *La Bayadère* Act II and *Madame Butterfly*, and I was dancing the lead and only male part in *Bayadère*. In rehearsals for *Bayadère*, I was trying to do a particularly difficult step, with the aim of making it better and more exciting than it had ever been. In keeping with my post-injury mentality, I was determined to show the younger boys a thing or two. I went a little too far, and on landing I heard a distinct *crunch* from my knee. *Oh god*, I thought, *please let it just be a meniscus or something and not the ACL.*

The company's Melbourne doctor Karim Khan took one look and said: 'Mmm, this isn't good.' He immediately took me to Olympic Park to see Peter Brukner, a sports medicine physician who treated a lot of AFL players – an ACL, or anterior cruciate ligament, rupture is a classic AFL injury. 'Oh my god, I've never seen one so fresh,' Peter said, looking at the looseness around the knee. And then the exact words I didn't want to hear: 'Yeah, it's definitely an ACL.' Karim, an amazing doctor and person, had an incredible bedside manner with the knack of being simultaneously funny and professional. Somehow he managed to make me laugh as I was sitting there absorbing this disastrous news.

A couple of years earlier, fellow principal dancer Nicole Rhodes had suffered almost exactly the same injury and had travelled to Sydney for surgery. On the surgeon's advice, the company then developed a new protocol for ACL injuries, which involved 'pre-hab', meaning a couple of weeks of strengthening work around the injury to allow the best and quickest possible recovery from surgery. I did the pre-hab, and by the time I went to Sydney to see the company's surgeon, I was walking quite easily on the leg, jogging and even running up and down stairs. I started to entertain a thought that perhaps it wasn't an ACL after all – but the specialist surgeon, Leo Pinczewski, immediately declared it a classic injury of that type, and I had surgery two weeks later in March. Basically, the surgery entailed stripping a piece of my hamstring, inserting it behind the kneecap where the anterior ligament was, and attaching it to both the tibia and femur with screws. Over time, the body amazingly turned the grafted tendon into a ligament. Quite magical really, but the bad news was that it would take six months for the graft to be stable, and then another six months to return to normal function. This meant no performing for another full year. It was a huge blow, but there was nothing to be done except deal with it and hope for the best recovery possible. The surgery went well, and the long, tedious rehabilitation began.

The thought of doing nothing but rehab for a year, and not performing, was like torture to me. I went to see Ian McRae, the company's general manager, and Maina, and begged them to give me things to do around the company that didn't require full use of the recovering ACL. Maina was wonderfully understanding throughout my years of injury – kind, positive and patient – and it meant the world to me to have her encouragement in that way. It also gave me a good model to follow when I took over the top job and had to manage injured dancers myself.

After I explained that a year on the sidelines doing rehab and watching *Oprah* (much as I loved to watch *Oprah*) might send me completely mad, Ian and Maina found a host of other roles for me to perform, including teaching a bit of warm-up barre, taking a couple of rehearsals for Robert Ray's *The Sentimental Bloke*, and also being the receptionist at the front desk when the real receptionists were on their lunchbreak. That job was so much harder than I ever could have imagined, and I still feel bad about all the people – there were quite a few – I accidentally disconnected.

The rehab was very time-consuming and demanding, kind of like rebuilding my whole body from the ground up, with particular focus on my injured knee. Being in my thirties – with very few male dancers still performing beyond their thirties – it was hard to avoid the obvious question of whether this would end my career. When my injury was fresh and I was still on crutches, I bumped into Steve Heathcote in the corridor and explained what had happened and the prognosis.

'Oh mate,' Steve said, sympathetically, 'what will you do? Will you quit?'

'Oh no,' I replied, 'I'm going to have the surgery; I'm going to come back.' I knew it was not a guarantee, but I was determined that my career was not going to end in this way. I would do everything in my power to recover and get back to dancing at full capacity. All of the medical staff were confident I'd be able to make a full recovery, too – the only concern was that a bad landing from a jump could jeopardise it.

At this time I also, rather importantly as it later turned out, started attending a lot of sponsorship functions, shadowing our head of corporate affairs, Kenneth Watkins, to pretty much any event that was on offer. The company always liked to have a dancer in tow to meet sponsors, and as I was an extrovert who liked talking to people, it was a very happy arrangement; I loved every minute of it. These events led me to spend a lot of time with Katie McLeish, a very beautiful and dynamic member of the sponsorship team – not a dancer as per my (once-broken) rule, but not far removed from dancing, either. I was drawn to her energy and intelligence. Soon we started spending time together away from work, and then we became lovers.

Once again, this was a period of great self-discovery, with Katie introducing me to life outside the 'ballet bubble' – a world of which I had very little experience – at a time when I was contemplating my future and what it might hold. While I was still very determined to get back on stage, I knew that even if I managed a full recovery, I couldn't dance forever, and I would eventually have to think about what to do with the rest of my life. I was very upfront with Katie about my relationship with Kelvin, as I didn't want there to be any secrets between us. As always, I loved being part of a couple and being involved in a new social set. It was great to have the emotional intimacy that comes with a relationship: being able to share my thoughts and feelings with someone, knowing they would take care of them. She also gave me brilliant, warm and fun companionship at a time when I was often separated from my ballet 'family' – who, for most dancers, are people that you spend more time with than your actual family.

It all came to an end with a big revelation around the dinner table. One evening, I had been invited to her share house for dinner. There were three couples: Katie's two housemates and their boyfriends, plus the two of us. It was a terrific night, made all the more enjoyable because I found myself able to hold conversations with non-ballet people and not feel like an outsider, but rather that thing I had always longed to be, even if I wasn't quite sure what it meant: a 'normal' person. We had all had a rather large amount of wine and a lot of laughs, when I looked across the table at one of the other men and thought, *My god, what a beautiful man*. It was then that the realisation struck me: I wasn't just admiring the guy's handsomeness; I was physically attracted to him, and I could see a future where being with a man would be the thing that would make me truly happy. How could I ever be in an honest, monogamous relationship with a woman?

I mulled over these thoughts, and the next day, once the wine-induced fog had lifted, I went for a long walk with Katie and told her about what had happened to me the night before, explaining that I needed to explore my attraction to men. As much as I had, over the years, entertained the thought of eventually marrying a woman and having children – a future that held a lot of appeal to me – I also didn't want to lead a double life. Katie was extremely understanding and kind that day, and her friendship has been another one that has endured.

With my head starting to sort itself out, there was still the issue of my ACL. It, too, was pulling itself together nicely and the rehab was going as expected. At one stage, Karim warned me that while the injury meant a year off stage, it would probably be more like eighteen months before the knee felt normal again, and as usual he was right. It was about halfway through 1996, with six months back on stage under my belt, when the realisation suddenly struck me that I hadn't thought about my knee all day. It still swelled up occasionally and I'd have to ice it and rest overnight, but it always returned to normal and I was able to dance as usual the next day.

I learnt a lot from my years of injury, particularly being off for such an extended time after the ACL surgery. I came to the realisation that I needed to have confidence in my dancing but not push myself too hard – none of this silly competing with the younger guys coming through. I was an older dancer now, bringing a maturity to my performance, but I also needed to face the physical reality that I couldn't do what I used to do. I decided to relax and not be paranoid about who could jump higher or do more pirouettes than I could. It was this new mindset that allowed me to keep dancing, injury-free, for several more years.

Around this time, the company itself was bracing for another upheaval: Maina's contract had not been renewed and she was leaving at the end of 1996. No one knew who the replacement artistic director would be, and for us older dancers, the question was: would they keep on the experienced principals, or sweep out the top ranks to shape it in their own vision?

My great personal hope, now that I was finally fully fit, was to continue my dance career for as long as my body allowed. I prayed that whoever took over the top job would see things the same way.

CHAPTER 7

Two endings ... and a beginning

Maina's departure wasn't a shock. We had known since 1994 that her contract ended in 1996 and that she would be leaving. At that time, the company was in a fractious phase, with lots of tension between dancers and management. Some dancers were unhappy with Maina's autocratic style, and a few of the company's brightest stars left. Lisa Pavane and Greg Horsman resigned; Miranda Coney and Adam Marchant took jobs with the highly regarded Nederlands Dans Theater. There was unease within the principal ranks, as was always the case when contemporaries felt they needed to leave – for those who stayed, it made questions about the viability of their own careers rise to the fore.

In addition, I think there was tension between Maina and the board, although the dancers were shielded from it. Strangely, once the decision was made for Maina to leave, she seemed to soften her approach somewhat, and the last two years of her directorship were, from my perspective at least, extremely happy ones. This was demonstrated in a tour of the United States in 1994, in which I danced opening night of *La Fille mal gardée* in Seattle and once again in *Don Quixote* at the Kennedy Center in Washington – one of the most memorable experiences of my performing career.

It was announced midway through 1996 that Ross Stretton would take over from Maina as artistic director at the beginning of 1997. It is hard to imagine two people more different from each other, either in style or approach to the company. Ross was born in Canberra in 1952, and was a champion tap dancer before switching to ballet at the relatively late age of seventeen. He took to it naturally, being long and lean and having that 'princely' look so revered in ballet's traditional aesthetic (the look that had tormented me for so long). He joined The Australian Ballet in the 1970s and became a principal before leaving for the United States to dance with the Joffrey Ballet and then the famous American Ballet Theatre. He retired from dancing in 1990 but stayed at American Ballet Theatre in administrative roles, becoming assistant director in 1993. He was an Australian with a lot of experience overseas, particularly with one of the most exciting and highly regarded companies in the world, and in addition, he had connections to a contemporary company of high repute in the Joffrey. While we didn't know Ross on a personal level, we certainly knew of him and had high hopes for his directorship.

Where Maina was very hands-on and involved in everything, Ross was far more remote, almost aloof. Maina loved being in the studio and was there pretty much all day teaching class and taking rehearsals. She would engage in conversations about anything and everything, usually at suppers after the show, and always encouraged us to approach her. In contrast, Ross was more a 'no news is good news' type – if you didn't hear from him, then everything was fine. It was a big shift for us all. By the time he arrived in Melbourne to take up the directorship, the senior ranks in the company were looking pretty thin. There were only three male principals left: me, Steven Heathcote and Li Cunxin, who had joined the company in 1995 from Houston Ballet after having been a guest artist a few times in past years. It was hard not to worry that Ross might clean out the ranks some more – a common response for many new directors.

I was turning thirty-four at the end of the year, and wondered if he might suggest I move along. It was a welcome surprise when Ross arrived and was extremely supportive of the three of us. In addition, he almost immediately promoted Damien Welch to principal to bolster the ranks. Damien was the son of two Australian Ballet founding principal dancers, Marilyn Jones and Garth Welch (and the brother of resident choreographer Stanton Welch), and had worked his way up through the company after training at The Australian Ballet School. When putting together a production, Ross had fewer casts than Maina and more dancers in roles according to their rank: principals danced principal roles, soloists danced soloist roles and so on. That first year, as we were getting to know each other, I was able to dance all the principal roles, which was a gift to me. But it was still an uncertain time when we were getting used to an artistic director who was nowhere near as visible, or approachable, as Maina – we felt like we'd gone from high school to university overnight, suddenly largely left to our own devices. Ross was an excellent and supportive teacher and gave brilliant classes, but there wasn't going to be any unnecessary communication or generally 'warm and fuzzy' feelings from Ross. It just wasn't his style.

Ross was determined to shake up the repertoire and bring in more contemporary works alongside the classics. This move, again, differed from Maina's approach and was always likely to ruffle feathers, which it surely did. He programmed lots of new repertoire, including, unsurprisingly, a broad range of American works, such as Agnes de Mille's *Fall River Legend* and Twyla Tharp's *In the Upper Room*. I was astonished to find that I was cast in both and danced just about every performance of *In the Upper Room* – I did not imagine I would be a choice for either of those, as I thought of myself as more of a classical than contemporary dancer.

The culture shock brought about by the change of directorship was pronounced. I had spent my whole career under Maina's leadership; I was used to her style and to her always *being there* – probably too much at times for some dancers, but it felt normal that she was heavily involved in every aspect of our working lives. She was always at a performance – we used to play a game of 'spot Maina' from the stage, which wasn't that hard as she usually sat in the same place at every show. Ross was sometimes there, sometimes not – we never knew. His approach was to do more of the external work – he was always out meeting with people, selling the company. This reflected the American model from which he came, and was something that had not happened to the same extent in Australia. Dancers are an anxious bunch and, at a time of upheaval, need a lot of positive reinforcement. Ross did not provide much, and instead left the pastoral care to his ballet staff. Some of the dancers interpreted his absence as evidence that he did not care. I was convinced this was not true, but that's how it felt to them.

Ross was a man of strong opinions, which he expressed with great conviction. His response to almost everything was to query, 'Why do we do it like that, and couldn't we do it this way instead?' It wasn't just the dancers that were shaken up – it was the entire company. Ross's appointment coincided with The Australian Ballet beginning an institutional change. The company had entered a corporatisation phase, beginning an evolution into a more modern outfit, with a stronger sponsorship and publicity arm. When Ross came in, he put a rocket under all of that as well, turning a company that he seemed to believe had long been stuck in its ways on its head. He undertook a major rebranding of the company and wanted us to be altogether sexier: where Maina had wanted us to be a traditional ballet company, Ross wanted us to be a broader dance company, more modern in outlook. It was a tumultuous time as he tried to make his grand vision come to fruition.

I enjoyed working with Ross. He always encouraged me, and he recognised that I did a lot of good work for him – I'd often fill in on shows if a dancer was injured, and he showed his appreciation by describing me as his 'go-to' man when he needed someone to step in and 'save' the show. One very memorable example was during a tour to Shanghai when I danced the opening night with fellow principal dancer Nicole Rhodes. The second night was our night off, and we had a booking at the famous restaurant M on the Bund for dinner. We were side stage waiting for the performance to start when the ballerina for that night pulled her calf. All around us were panic stations. Nicole and I went on to dance Act II and III, which was quite unusual, particularly as we had danced the night before. The show must always go on. Thankfully, we did have that dinner the following night.

It was one of the most productive periods of my career, and I managed to stay relatively injury-free until I retired. Having said that, I was still battling my tendency to look over my shoulder, at times to the point of paranoia. When we were rehearsing for *Swan Lake*, I noticed that I was only cast for two shows while all the other principals had three, so I asked Ross about it. 'Oh, I don't have three shows for everyone; it has to be this way,' he said. And then added: 'If there's a problem, I'll talk to you.' That was a relief – no need to decode the cast sheets with Ross.

There were the inevitable blows, too. The biggest one was when Ross invited Natalia Makarova – one of the 20th century's greatest ballerinas – to stage her version of *La Bayadère* in 1998. She sent her assistant choreographer Olga Evreinoff to set the ballet, which entailed doing an initial casting, with input from Ross and the ballet staff, and teaching all the steps prior to Makarova's arrival. Olga had cast me as Solor – the male lead – paired with Nicole Rhodes. I was feeling pretty happy with myself. There were about five casts and the rehearsals seemed to go well – as usual, all the dancers were jockeying to be in good shape for a plum casting once Makarova arrived.

About two weeks before opening night, the great former ballerina arrived and started to look at the casts – an audition, in effect. She immediately moved things around and broke up casts to create new ones, which is not unusual for a choreographer. But in the process, she moved Nicole to first cast and I was ... nowhere. I had been dumped as Solor. Instead, she cast me as the Bronze Idol – a character role that has a spectacular solo in the last act, but is definitely not a lead.

I'm not sure if it was my 'look' that didn't appeal to Makarova or if I wasn't her kind of dancer, but I was gutted, and it tapped into all my old insecurities. Was I not tall, handsome or princely enough to be Solor? Or was it that I was too old? Around and around in my head these questions went. Finally, I reached my usual default setting in situations like these that enabled me to accept the decision: that was 'showing her' and rehearsing extra hard, making sure I was the best damned Bronze Idol the world had ever seen. I danced my heart out on opening night, and so many people commented on my performance afterwards – 'Oh my god, that was amazing!' – that I joked that I would paint myself gold more often, as that was how you got noticed. Even Makarova came backstage after the show and said to me, 'Oh, that was so good – you should look at doing Solor.' I succeeded at not screaming in frustration, but at the same time felt vindicated that I was good enough to do what she had taken away from me.

This experience sent me a message that I couldn't ignore – my dance career was coming to an end, even if it was happening slowly, and I had to think about something I really never wanted to think about: a life after performing. In the back of my mind, and for tiny moments in the front of it, I started to imagine what that might look like. It also made me determined to continue dancing for as long as I could, and happily I was still being given most of the male lead roles.

I continued to receive generally positive reviews. As a performer, reviews are a double-edged sword: you want to believe the good ones, but you also want to believe that the less favourable ones were a mistake, that the reviewer was wrong or just didn't *get* what you were trying to do. You can't have it both ways. When I started my career, all that mattered were the print reviews – there was no online news and no social media to worry about. Newspapers were king, and we all read what was written about us. The reviews were posted on a noticeboard in the cafeteria, so everyone could see them, even the bad ones. (When I became artistic director, one of the first things the dancers asked me was to stop this practice, as it felt to them like a kind of public shaming.)

Some reviews I received – especially early in my career – put me on a high for weeks. With the flood of attention Liz and I received from our Moscow trip came a lot of effusive reviews. Then there was a bit of a backlash, too, in that Australian way, as there was probably a perception that we were getting a little full of ourselves.

One of my favourite reviews of all time was this one from that magical night dancing *Coppélia* for Princess Diana in 1992. Edward Thorpe wrote in the *Evening Standard*: 'David McAllister, as her lover, Franz, scored several personal successes when the company was last here four years ago and is dancing now with undiminished brio and virtuosity so necessary to the Franz character.'

And at the other end of the scale, this one stuck in my mind, too, from Patricia Laughlin at *Dance Australia* magazine. It was 1988 and we were doing *The Three Musketeers*, in which I was dancing one of the musketeers but also, in another performance, the role of D'Artagnan. Laughlin wrote: 'David McAllister gives almost no attention to interpretation and as a result I have no impression at all of his character of Athos.'

Sometimes the reviewer is right, and you know you haven't had a good show. Even when I thought a review was unfair, my modus operandi was always to prove the person wrong, so sometimes poor reviews can really work to motivate you. As I said, if you want to believe the good ones, you have to believe the less flattering ones, too – there's an element of truth in them all.

Generally, my ego held up pretty well under the strain of reviews – I cared much more about what Maina or Ross thought of me and the reception the audience gave on the night. At that time, there was nowhere near the focus on mental health and well-being that there is now; they were not even terms in our lexicon.

Dealing with pain – physical or psychological – was all part of what was required of us, and mostly, we kept it to ourselves. In the early days, smoking was also a favoured way of dealing with stress – and it had the added bonus of suppressing appetite. In addition to this, the ballet company was sponsored by the cigarette brand Benson & Hedges, so they were easy for us to come by. (Can you imagine announcing such a partnership now?) In the 1980s, people smoked freely in class. I remember that Paul de Masson actually had an empty Milo tin nailed to the wall that he used as a makeshift ashtray during rehearsals. It seems utterly outrageous from today's viewpoint, but back then no one thought anything of it.

Among the most important bolsters to my well-being throughout my career were the amazing women I danced with. Doing a ballet with someone is a special kind of intimacy – so often you are telling a love story, frequently with a tragic twist, and you and your partner need to approach the ballet from the same perspective in order for the audience to believe the story you are portraying. Apart from Liz, with whom I had a magical connection, I was partnered with several women who brought out the best in me as a dancer and as an actor. In my early years in the company, I was often paired with Fiona Tonkin and Joady Chambers, who were both fantastic partners. Joady sadly danced for only a short time because she was keen to explore life beyond ballet, but performing with her was always electric – she had such innate theatricality and charm. Fiona unlocked some of the repertoire that I felt I may not have been able to dance otherwise, and it was always a joy to share the stage with her.

One of my most unlikely couplings was with the very beautiful ballerina Justine Summers. We were paired to dance the third act pas de deux from *The Sleeping Beauty* in Beijing in 1996. Justine was an exquisite dancer, but *en pointe* and wearing a tiara was a good 20 centimetres taller than I was. That same year, we were invited to Singapore to dance the second act pas de deux from *La Sylphide* in a gala with the Singapore Dance Theatre. This was a much more successful repertoire choice, as it required us to dance alongside each other, unlike the *Sleeping Beauty* performance in which I was standing behind her for a lot of the time. I loved dancing with Justine, but I think it made much more sense when she returned to dancing with the taller Steven Heathcote.

During the 1990s, I also danced regularly with the fabulously talented Vicki Attard. I performed my very first Siegfried in Anne Woolliams's *Swan Lake* with Vicki in 1991. After nine years of dancing the ballet in smaller roles, I finally cracked it for a shot at Siegfried. This was the ballet that made me feel like I'd really 'arrived' as a principal. Vicki, who was clearly extremely talented, was a newly promoted soloist (later also a principal), so we had a great time discovering the most famous ballet of them all together. We worked so well together because of our great mutual respect and our love of inhabiting the roles we were dancing, not just physically but also emotionally, really making them believable. I will never forget the first performance we did together of *Swan Lake* – Vicki had such a badly strained neck that she could hardly turn her head, and even had to get one of the other dancers to put her hair into a bun for her. That didn't stop her from putting in a luminous performance, even managing twenty-four consecutive *fouettés* (where the dancer extends her leg to the side then whips it around into a pirouette *en pointe*, then lands with her leg to the side and does it all again, without stopping), which must have been agony with her stiff neck.

Vicki had extraordinary stamina and rehearsed extensively in order to have every detail finessed and ready for the performance, whereas I was more inclined to see what the vibe was like on the night and be open to making small changes if it felt right. Working with her taught me to enjoy rehearsing in minute detail, and I hope in return I gave her the confidence to throw caution to the wind occasionally and take risks on stage. We danced the opening night of *Romeo and Juliet* together in Melbourne in 1997, which was something I never thought I would do. My usual role in *Romeo and Juliet* opening night was Mercutio, but Ross changed things up for his first season as director, and it was a huge honour to perform the role of Romeo. The performance was a personal highlight, and it was a joy to be out there with Vicki for the premiere in Melbourne. It was also something of a learning experience. After the show, I expressed to Ross what an honour it was to be performing the opening night as Romeo, but that I felt I made a better Mercutio. He must have agreed, as in Sydney he changed the cast. Another very special collaboration with Vicki was choreographer Stephen Baynes's pas de deux *El Tango* that he created for us. It was sexy, slinky and a huge change of pace, and I loved every minute of performing it.

Miranda Coney was another partner who was important to my dance career. Like me, Miranda was from Perth, where she had trained with renowned teacher Diana Waldron, who also ran Perth City Ballet, which provided young dancers with lots of opportunities to perform. I remember seeing Miranda dance when she was about nine years old – she was in a choreographic competition and must have been one of the youngest entrants, but her determination and great potential really stood out. Our paths next crossed when she came to The Australian Ballet School and danced the role of Kitri as a first-year student in the Dryad scene from *Don Quixote* at the end-of-year performance. She managed to be delicate and extremely strong at the same time – a very mature level of performance for such a young dancer. In the company, we were often paired together, to my delight. I felt our most memorable performances were the *Coppélia* with Princess Diana in the audience, and my final performance, which was *Giselle*. Miranda was my partner in that performance, and I was thrilled to share this with her, as she was one of The Australian Ballet's great Giselles.

While I danced with many supremely talented ballerinas in my career, there were three others who were particularly vital to the success of my final years in the company: Nicole Rhodes, Simone Goldsmith and Madeleine Eastoe. Nicole and I were a great match, as her energy and power on stage was a great boost to me as I entered the twilight of my career.

Simone's star was still rising as mine was fading, but Ross recognised her ability and paired us in *Manon* and the revival of Stanton Welch's *Madame Butterfly*. It was especially satisfying to dance *Butterfly* after having missed the original season through injury, and Simone was the embodiment of this ballet, as she had been there from the creation of the work. Each time I joined Simone on stage was an experience to be treasured. It was especially gratifying to see her continue to blossom in my first years as artistic director.

The experience of dancing with the last of my great partners was a very short-lived but wonderfully intense time on stage with Madeleine. I remember noticing Maddie when she joined the company and thinking I really wanted to dance with her – fortunately, that happened very quickly. We were cast in George Balanchine's *Tchaikovsky Pas de Deux.* Dancing with Maddie was an unmitigated joy: her innate musicality and buoyant technique perfectly matched the way I danced. She was also tiny, and I remember thinking after those first shows that if only I were ten years younger, we could have been a great pairing with longevity.

Ah yes, if only I were ten years younger. That thought was swirling in my head as we entered the final years of the 1990s, and I wondered how much longer I could dance and what I would do when the curtain inevitably came down. In 1999, Adrian Burnett, a senior artist and choreographer with The Australian Ballet, told me he was applying to Deakin University to study arts administration. I knew I needed to do something text-based and intellectual after all those years of kinetic learning, so I enrolled, too. Even though I didn't want to be in administration – I didn't want to be a general manager – I thought the Deakin course would teach me more about the business side of arts companies, how they operate, who controls what and so on. I hadn't done any study like that since school. I bought myself a computer and set about trying to reawaken a dormant part of my brain.

Slowly, I was cobbling together a plan for life after ballet. Maina had planted a seed in my mind in 1996, when she spoke to me in one of the exit interviews she had with everyone as she left the company. In our conversation, she said to me: 'You know, I can imagine you directing a company at some point,' to which I replied, 'Oh, gosh, I'd really love that.' She added: 'And I think you'd make a great ballet master as well.' Being a teacher in a ballet company as she suggested also sounded terrific to me. Along with the study, I thought perhaps Maina might be able to help me make connections with influential people when it came time for me to retire, given she was at that point in Denmark and was then heading to Boston.

I was hoping Ross would allow me to stay on as a dancer until 2001, my twentieth year in the company. After that, as I edged towards forty, I knew I would need to look at retiring. I planned to pursue teaching in an international dance company, and would probably do a teaching course to help me do that. While I was on tour with the company in the United States in 1999, I travelled to Hartford, Connecticut, where there was a teacher training course that had established a great reputation. I thought this course might be the ideal one to look into as my plan to become a ballet master started taking shape. I hoped that this might then lead to being appointed an assistant director and then, perhaps, a director. It was all a bit vague, but it gave me something to strive for instead of staring into the abyss of life after dancing.

But that plan changed very quickly. At the beginning of 2000, as we all came back to work for a new year, Ross announced he had been appointed director of The Royal Ballet in London and was leaving. None of us dancers had any idea this was coming, and we were shocked. We had been to New York in October and had a wonderful season, and we had a number of exciting events planned around the Sydney Olympics in 2000, so the whole company had been on a high before the summer break.

In terms of the artistic directorship, the vacancy opening up at this point felt like a bit of a blow – it was too early for me. I was one year into my study and had a full year to go, and at the time of the announcement, my headspace was still very much that of a dancer. But as the press reports about Ross's departure came out, there was mention of me as a possible replacement. (I suspected this had been planted by Noel Pelly, a huge supporter of mine, and found out years later that this was in fact true.) This put me into a quandary – maybe I should throw my hat in the ring after all, just for the experience if nothing else?

I spoke to Ian McRae, the company's general manager, who was enthusiastic but cautious: he suggested that perhaps the deputy role would be a better one for me to aim for at this stage. 'Oh, I don't think I'll get it,' I told him. 'It's just because I'm doing all this study and it would be really good for me to try to put some of it into practice.' The thought of being a deputy was exciting – I assured him I would love that job. 'But,' I added, 'are you even looking for one? Or only an artistic director?' At the time they were not – it was the directorship or nothing.

I couldn't shake the little buzz of excitement that had lodged itself in my mind. I sounded out the company's chairman, Mel Ward, who said more or less the same thing Ian had: I probably needed more qualifications for the top job. I decided to talk to Noel Pelly – who had always been a mentor to me – to see if it was worthwhile applying. Noel knew all there was to know about The Australian Ballet, having been with the company since its inception. As the publicist in 1962, he wrote the very first press release about the company's founding. Being a trained lawyer, he rose through the ranks to become general manager, a role he held until he retired. In many ways, Noel was the company's heart and soul. He gave me the advice I wanted to hear: 'You've got nothing to lose; just do it!' He then helped me put together an application, something I had next to no experience with, having basically auditioned for every position I'd ever held. Clearly a two-minute solo from *Don Quixote* wasn't going to cut it on this occasion. Firstly, Noel told me to gather letters of support from as many 'big names' in ballet as I could, so I asked three renowned choreographers – Glen Tetley, Peter Wright and Graeme Murphy – and they obliged.

I rang Graeme first, because I thought that if he was going to apply then I wouldn't. I did the same with John Meehan, a choreographer and well-known former Australian Ballet principal dancer. Both said they were not applying, so I forged ahead.

I was desperate for the next director to be someone deeply passionate about the company and its future, so I thought: *Here we go*, took a deep breath and started the arduous task of assembling my application. The recruitment consultant charged with finding the new director suggested that, to offset my lack of experience, I should put together a 'vision statement' to explain what I would like to do with the company, how I would like to shape its destiny. This seemed like an excellent idea.

In a nutshell, my pitch was this: I wanted to build the 'Australian-ness' of the company by fostering talent and commissioning new Australian works. I would also engage with a new generation of choreographers, commissioning works from those on their way up as well as those already established; strengthen our international reputation; and pay tribute to our past while building a strong future for a company in which all dancers could thrive.

While I was deeply absorbed in all of this, I received a phone call from my dad. Mum was very sick in hospital, and I needed to come home immediately. Although getting this call was something I had been half-expecting for some time, it was nonetheless a deep shock when it actually happened. In 1998, two years earlier, Mum had been diagnosed with chronic myeloid leukaemia. Initially, the prognosis had not been particularly grim: she was part of a drug trial that had proved very successful, bringing her blood count back to normal and effectively putting her into remission. Before her diagnosis, she had been feeling sick for a while – it had taken some time for leukaemia to be diagnosed – so this was a huge improvement for her, and we were all feeling optimistic that she had several more years of life to enjoy. The doctors were also quite bullish, telling us that given the drugs were working so well, it was possible for people to live for twenty years with the disease.

She stayed well for about a year, long enough to see my sister, Di, get married. Mum became tired more easily than she had before, but generally she seemed to be doing very well. I went home to see her at Christmas in 1998 and then again in 1999, and although on the later occasion she'd had a bit of a hiccup with her health, she recovered and seemed to be better again.

Then early in 2000, she developed pleurisy, but again seemed to recover well. Not long after that, her legs started to swell all the time, and she was admitted to hospital. The doctors treated this successfully, but further testing revealed that her leukaemia had gone from 'chronic' to 'acute', which was devastating news. It meant the disease had come back with a vengeance, and had really taken hold. The doctors gave her and Dad some options, but warned them that these secondary illnesses would keep happening at shorter and shorter intervals. Eventually, her body would no longer be able to fight them and it would become a palliative situation. The alternative was an aggressive chemotherapy regimen, with the aim of killing off all the 'bad' cells and allowing her body to generate new, healthy ones.

She wanted to fight on – my sister had just fallen pregnant and Mum was excited about the arrival of her first grandchild – so she chose the chemo. She started with the aggressive chemo regimen and for a few months she seemed to respond very well. The treatment took her to the point of having no immunity in order to kill off the 'rogue' blood cells; it was at this point the pleurisy returned and she became critically ill. That was when Dad called me and told me to come home.

Around the time of Mum's diagnosis, my younger brother Paul had come out to our family as being gay. While there was no question that our parents loved us, it was a bit of a surprise. As my mum said to me, 'I always thought it would be you.' Sadly, I had not been able to do that just yet. I was still, after all these years, wrestling with my sexuality. I had been seeing some men, casually, but I was not in a relationship – deliberately so. I was really happy for Paul – he had met his partner, Steve, and was ready to share the news with the family. I was not at that stage, and would never have that conversation with my mum.

The application for the artistic directorship was due the following week. Not knowing how long I would be there, I hurriedly packed a bag with a couple of changes of clothes and my laptop, and flew home to Perth. When I arrived, the doctors did not paint an entirely bleak picture, even though her situation was clearly critical. She was barely recognisable to me, tiny in her hospital bed, attached to a respirator. I stayed with her late one night. Because of the respirator, she couldn't speak or eat and her mouth was horribly dry, so I just sat next to her and ran ice cubes over her lips, trying to hydrate her a little. It was clear that our dear mum, who had done so much for us, taught us so many things and loved us so deeply, was slipping away. 'Mum,' I whispered to her, 'we're going to be fine. If you need to go, it's okay, you can go.' It was one of the hardest nights of my life.

The archbishop came to see Mum a couple of days after I arrived and gave her the blessing of the sick, and the next day, almost inconceivably, she was off the respirator and her vital signs were improving. Perhaps, we thought, she'll pull through again. I spent many hours in the hospital room while she slept, tapping away at my application on my laptop. She seemed to be on the way back, so I explained to her that I needed to return to Melbourne, to which she replied, 'Yes, that's fine.'

I boarded a plane to Melbourne feeling relatively positive – she was still gravely ill, but I thought she would pull through. She was knitting a blanket for me and kept trying to work on it, even though the medical staff told her not to worry about it. She was determined to finish it, but her body was not cooperating. The next day her health deteriorated again, and she fell into a coma.

I got home to Melbourne just in time to meet the application cut-off date – I delivered it in person because the post would have been too slow. The following day, Dad rang to say that Mum had died. I got straight back on a plane to Perth. Because I hadn't been there when she'd taken her last breath, I told Dad I wanted to see her; I just needed to know that it was real.

Before a rosary that had been organised prior to the funeral, Mum was in an open coffin for the family to view. I was in for a shock. Her hair had been shaved off because it had been falling out due to the chemotherapy, but the wig that was ordered hadn't arrived in time. She was dressed in her best outfit that she'd worn to my sister's wedding, and had heaps of make-up on her, so the end result was that she looked a bit like Uncle Fester from the Addams Family. *Well, I know that's Mum but it doesn't look like Mum*, I thought. Nonetheless, it was important for me to see her in a coffin, to know that she was really gone, and to say a final goodbye.

In keeping with her faith, there was a full Requiem Mass funeral. The church was packed, which was very moving and a great comment on the impact Mum had on her friends and the community. I spoke along with my brothers and sister, though I have no memory at all of what I said. The weeks leading up to this had been such a blur of high emotion: the excitement of handing in my application, the stress and worry and then grief about Mum. After the funeral there was a wake, and a stream of people from my childhood came up to speak to me. It was wonderful and strange, as they all seemed the same yet older, while I felt I hadn't aged at all. I had decided not to take communion, even though I knew my mum would have wanted me to. I couldn't square it with myself, given that I hadn't been to church in years. I stayed noticeably seated while the others had communion, all of us trying, and succeeding mostly, to be stoic. Dad in particular was a tower of strength, despite being shattered by Mum's death – theirs had been a long and devoted partnership.

It may sound a little strange, but I really wish I had a video of my mum's funeral – like we have of my sister's wedding – so I could watch it again and again. I remember so very little of it, just the huge tangle of emotions. A parent dying, no matter your relationship with them (mine thankfully had been wonderfully loving), is such a pivotal moment in a person's life, and I wish I had a way to process it all properly and enjoy everything people said about my mum in the service. I was very touched that my friend Margaret Bourke flew over to represent all my friends who couldn't be there. As always through the tough times in my life, she was a great source of strength for me.

A few days later, I made the trip back east to Melbourne, having temporarily put the prospect of the artistic directorship to one side. I was still a principal dancer and we were performing, so I needed to return for rehearsals. The trouble was my back was hurting, which I attributed to not attending classes for a couple of weeks. I went to see Sue Mayes, the company's physiotherapist, who examined me but couldn't find anything wrong – no real physical symptoms. 'I think you should go and talk to our psychologist,' she suggested. I went immediately and was given some wonderful advice: 'You've had a major trauma. Your central nervous system is part of your back, and your back is your central support. You've just lost your mother, who's been an incredible central support to you in your life. This is probably your body trying to deal with your grief.' Literally from that moment, my back was fine. I returned to class and rehearsal, keeping largely to myself the fact that I had applied to lead the company, and continued preparing to perform while trying to process my mother's death. It was a crazy, emotionally turbulent time.

Things moved along swiftly with the artistic directorship. I was interviewed by the recruitment company and then had a second with a smaller group from the board – the selection panel. The recruitment company pulled together a short list of suitable candidates, then the selection panel interviewed, assessed and made a recommendation to the board. I had no idea, really, if I was in with a shot, but as the process went on and I kept being called back, a tiny flame of excitement flared up. Could I possibly, actually, be the one?

The day before the August board meeting, Ian McRae found me. 'There's a board meeting tomorrow; they might want to meet with you,' he advised, which I think was his way of saying 'wear something nice', because in those days I'd go to work mostly in jeans and a T-shirt. The next morning, I arrived at work wearing the clothes I had bought to wear to my mum's funeral. I was thinking this was all part of the process, that there might be two preferred candidates and that we would both meet with the entire board. I arrived at 9 am, which to me felt like the crack of dawn, as our classes didn't begin until 10.30 and we had had a performance the night before.

I found Ian's executive assistant, who told me he was in the board meeting and she didn't know when he would be out. This was confusing as I thought I was expected to go to the meeting, but I wandered off and decided to warm up while I waited, to give myself something to do as much as anything. I changed out of my 'good' clothes and into warm-up gear, and was sitting doing some exercises on the studio floor when Ian stuck his head around the door. 'The chairman wants to meet with you in front of the theatre,' he told me. I quickly got changed again and, with my heart racing, went to meet Mel Ward.

I apologised to Mel when I found him; I was feeling a little frazzled and worried I had kept him waiting. 'No, that's fine,' he replied. 'Let's go and get a coffee.' I started to think it was not good news: *He's taking me away from the building so if I get upset and cry or anything, no one will see and it won't be so humiliating for me.* We walked towards Southbank and I inwardly assumed the brace position.

Mel cleared his throat. 'As you know, we've conducted a big international search ...'

Oh Jesus, Mel, I thought, *just tell me.*

'Look, to cut to the chase,' he eventually said, 'we'd like to offer you the job.' I had to stop walking. I thought my legs – those stocky old friends of mine – were going to give way completely. 'Oh my god,' I said to him. 'Oh ... Wow!'

'Is that not what you were expecting?' Mel asked, quite reasonably.

'Well, I'm delighted but ... this is real!' I replied.

We got to the cafe and I sat down, still feeling like my entire body was barely able to hold me up. Mel said, 'Here's the contract and here's the press release; I'll let you read for five minutes.' I read everything and told him it looked great. 'Well, I have to ask you,' Mel said, 'will you accept?' Would I? Would I accept the chance to have this great passion of mine be the opportunity to shape the national ballet company I loved so much? You bet I would.

'Great, so this is what we're going to do,' he continued. 'At 2.30 pm we'll call a company meeting to make the announcement, and then at 3 o'clock we'll go straight to a press conference, because we don't want this to leak; we want it all out at once. Okay?' At this point, we both realised that neither of us had any money to pay for the coffees, so Mel went back to the Ballet Centre to get some while I sat there trying to absorb the enormity of the news he'd just given me.

While sitting there, I remembered I had a stage call for Jiří Kylián's *Bella Figura* – Jiří would be there and I couldn't miss it. I thought it would probably be over by 2.30 pm, so I pushed it back in my mind. I sat reading the press release over and over, muttering *What the fuck* to myself and thinking a thousand terrified and excited thoughts about how I was going to make all this happen. I think if I knew then what I know now, I would have been even more nervous. As was noted in one newspaper at the time, I hadn't even run a 'chook raffle' and here I was being appointed to lead one of the premier arts companies in the country! Ignorance was bliss. I had half-finished my arts management course and had spent my career wholly at The Australian Ballet – not a bulging CV. But deep down I knew this was something I could do; it felt right and, weirdly, almost inevitable. I knew there was so much to learn, but I was willing to work day and night to achieve the dreams I had for the company. The dancers were wonderful, the organisation was strong and I was ready – a bit daunted, but ready.

Mel returned and paid for the coffees, and then I went and completed a warm-up before going to the rehearsal, where there was a lot of buzz about the 2.30 pm meeting. What was it about? Would it be the new director? I said nothing and tried to concentrate on the rehearsal. After the stage call, I got changed into my 'good' clothes once again and went to the meeting. 'Just hang back a bit,' Mel advised when I got there, so I stood at the back as the dancers and the entire staff filed into the studio.

After a short preamble, Mel said: 'I'm delighted to announce that the new artistic director is David McAllister.' There was an immediate reaction, possibly initially shock followed by a roar of applause and loud *woo-hooing* that lasted for what seemed like several minutes. The dancers and staff appeared happy, and I was over the moon. There I stood in my best threads, suddenly catapulted into this new role leading my erstwhile colleagues and friends, who were clapping and cheering my appointment. It was utterly euphoric, and as I looked out into that sea of dancers, I told myself: *Enjoy this moment, because in a year's time, they're going to hate your guts.* But for those minutes, they were excited that it would be one of their own taking over next year. And as we left the room that day, several of them came up to congratulate me, and ask the same question over and over: 'Can we still call you "Daisy"?' I hadn't even thought that far ahead; everything had been such a blur. But in a moment of clarity I replied: 'No, I think you will have to call me "Mr Daisy" now.'

CHAPTER 8

The curtain falls, and rises again

Suddenly, the post-dancing life I had spent so much time worrying about was brighter, more spectacular and more terrifying than I had envisaged. I was offered the role of artistic director in August 2000 and wasn't taking the reins until July 2001, almost a year away. Until then, Ross was still in charge.

Ross's tenure at the top had been tumultuous and continued that way even after he announced his departure. He had pushed the whole organisation out of its comfort zone, including the board, and it was no secret he had clashed with some dancers over his management style. His repertoire choices continued to be controversial for some, but also excited many others. He was his own man and doggedly believed in what he was doing for the company; if he ruffled feathers along the way, that was no problem. He was always kind and supportive to me as a dancer, for which I was extremely grateful, but I got the distinct feeling he wasn't too thrilled about my appointment as the incoming artistic director.

Immediately after my appointment was announced, I was asked to attend administration meetings as well as continue as a principal dancer, and Ross made sure, right from the start, that I knew my place. 'I'm still in charge and don't think you're running this company,' he said. 'There can't be two artistic directors; there's only one.' He had a very strong personality and I had no intention of treading on his toes – I had been dropped into a very large job for which I had relatively little experience, and was desperate to learn as much as I could, as quickly as possible.

Consequently, I sat down with him soon after my appointment and asked for his advice. 'Ross, you know this job better than anyone,' I began, 'and I've got a year to learn it.' Actually, at the time it was looking like it would be even longer, because he wanted to keep his tenure until the end of 2001, while starting with The Royal Ballet in September of the same year and effectively running two companies at once. The board eventually kyboshed this, and set the changeover date at midyear.

'I'd like to really pick your brains about how to do this,' I continued. But he wasn't interested in that. 'Look, everyone does this job differently; you'll do it differently from what I do and you won't really have any understanding of it until you put your feet under the desk.' I remember at the time feeling a bit shattered by this – *Thanks for nothing*, I thought. But in hindsight, I can see what he meant: we were very different characters and he was telling me to figure it out for myself, which was probably sage advice.

There were plenty of people who helped me, though. Foremost was general manager Ian McRae, who had become a mentor and almost a father-figure to me. Mel Ward, the chair who had appointed me, was also extremely supportive. Shortly after my appointment was announced, Mel said to me: 'Look, because of your inexperience, we think it's really important for you to have a deputy.' There was only one choice: Danny Radojevic. Danny was our ballet master and had joined the company at Ross's invitation. After winning a gold medal in Moscow while still a dancer with The Australian Ballet, he had spent the bulk of his career at American Ballet Theatre. Danny was a wonderful teacher and coach, and I knew he was the best person for the deputy's job. I spoke to him very soon after my appointment and was delighted when he accepted the role.

Having the old and new directors existing side by side was a bit confusing for everyone else as well. It was a strange time of people wanting to talk to me about my plans and their careers, but of me having to stress that Ross was still in charge, that he remained their first port of call – unless it related to something after July 2001, in which case I was their man.

The midyear changeover meant Ross and I also had to wrangle over the dancer intake and repertoire for 2001. The 1999 Nugent report – the federal government's major performing arts inquiry – had given the company enough money to hire ten more dancers, which would mean we went from a company of sixty-two to seventy-two. One of our arguments for this in our submission to the government was that it would allow us to do split touring – to effectively have two companies performing at once – which would be great for the company's international 'brand' and allow for a wider repertoire. But rather than take on ten new dancers all at once, we decided to hire five in the first year and another five in the second.

At the same time, dancers were leaving. Some had been planning to leave anyway, some were finished with dancing, and there is always a big turnover with an incoming artistic director as dancers, quite understandably, take stock of their careers and how they might fare under the new boss. A few approached me and told me that it wasn't about me; it was simply the right time for them to move on. I was often disappointed but understood. With the extra numbers we were able to employ and taking into account these resignations, this meant Ross and I had about twelve new contracts to offer for 2001.

This precipitated a pretty intense bartering period, because we wanted different dancers – not always, but often. He'd say: 'I want this one, this one and this one,' and I'd reply: 'Yeah, not so mad on this one but I really want that one,' and so on. It was a very open and professional conversation, but certainly had its moments of tension. I was conscious of the need to be completely transparent with him about everything. Because of the 'two boss' scenario, I wanted to be very clear that we were both on the same page and ensure there wasn't a possibility of us being played off against each other.

Shortly afterwards, Ross came to me about the schedule he had prepared for the 2001 season; he wanted to include *La Fille mal gardée*. I pushed back: it felt as though he was trying to pigeonhole my first months in charge by scheduling a ballet that I had been closely aligned with, and I knew he would never have programmed that ballet during his tenure. We reached agreement by replacing it with a mixed program that I felt more comfortable with. Then, after we had officially launched the season, which featured Harald Lander's *Études* in Ross's half of the year, the company received documentation saying we couldn't do *Études* because there wasn't a ballet master or mistress available to teach and stage the ballet at that time. Ross came to me with this problem, and we were able to rearrange the season a bit: he took Stephen Baynes's *Beyond Bach* into his half of the year, and I took *Études* into mine. My first program for the company was *Études*, Stanton Welch's *Divergence* and another piece Baynes had done for the Olympics called

Personal Best. It turned out to be an exciting but physically tough program, and one we had to live with.

As tricky as this time was in terms of dealing with Ross, I think he remembered that I had always been his 'go-to' dancer and agreed to fill in for others on many occasions, and I know he appreciated it. 'Oh gosh, you're my saviour,' he would say. When it came time to talk with him and the executive team about my final dancing performance, Ross was extremely generous. I had originally thought I would just stop at the end of the 2000 season, but he insisted that I have a bigger farewell. 'We'll do Melbourne and then Sydney and *Giselle* will be your final performance, and then you can go,' he said. He made it into a really important event for the company, and I was very touched and grateful.

In March 2001, I went on to the Sydney Opera House stage to dance *Giselle*, my last performance as a dancer with the company. I could not have wished for a more perfect Giselle to dance with than Miranda Coney, and the whole evening was better than any expectation I ever had – like the most exhausting, exhilarating and emotional roller-coaster you could ride. At the end, I walked forward with the white rose in my hand that Giselle had just passed from the grave, and it was as if the years on stage had melded into that one second. I was expecting a rush of emotion, possibly floods of tears, but actually there was just a huge feeling of joy and gratitude. I had had the most amazing experiences of my life each time the curtain lifted, in that magical place beyond the proscenium arch. It was the most poignant and personal moment suspended in time, but then the warmth of the applause brought me back to reality, with people standing, my family and friends and my wider 'ballet family' in the audience. I stood there wrapped in streamers, with the most beautiful bouquet of flowers, just drinking in the moment. It was like being showered with love. But even in that moment, I couldn't wait to step into the artistic directorship. I was elated at my farewell but exhilarated by what was ahead.

There were still a few months before I formally started in the job. The board had decided, very sensibly, to send me on an international immersion trip to basically learn the skills to be an artistic director. The aim was to make a clean break between my dance career and my managerial career, as well as allow Ross to serve out his tenure without me hovering in the wings. This plan was the brainchild of board member John Calvert-Jones, who provided the funding that enabled me to connect with key people abroad for advice and direction.

I spent seven weeks overseas, and had an extraordinary learning experience, meeting with Sir Anthony Dowell at The Royal Ballet in London, and Kevin McKenzie, artistic director with American Ballet Theatre. Both had been dancers in the companies that they then went on to direct, as I was about to do, so their insights were both generous and invaluable. I travelled to the Pacific Northwest Ballet in Seattle, where I spent time with Kent Stowell and Francia Russell, that company's founding directors. I was particularly keen to see them because they had worked with George Balanchine and performed a lot of his repertoire – as a Balanchine fan, I was keen to inject more of his work into our own upcoming program. They had also been such generous hosts to the company when we had toured there in 1994.

I went to see Petter Jacobsson at the Royal Swedish Ballet, as he had also been a dancer with that company, then danced in Birmingham before returning to the Royal Swedish Ballet as its director. I made my way to Birmingham Royal Ballet as well, because David Bintley, the artistic director, had been in the company before transitioning to artistic director – although he'd had a period as a choreographer. You can see there was a bit of a theme in my choice of places to visit, but essentially I saw as many people as I could, especially those who had made the move from dancer to director within the same company. Though it's not an unusual move in itself, it is rare to go straight from one to the other without working on something else in between. I was eager to glean as many tips as I could.

Already, my mind was turning to the choreographers I could possibly work with – I knew that this would be a pivotal part of my success (or otherwise) as a director. While I was in Europe, I arranged to meet John Neumeier, the director of the Hamburg Ballet and one of the world's pre-eminent choreographers. John is something of a legend in the ballet world, a prolific dance-maker and the director at Hamburg – incredibly – since 1973. I felt there was a hole in our repertoire at The Australian Ballet because we didn't have any Neumeier works, yet we had something from pretty much every other major choreographer in the world.

I saw John's production of *Nijinsky* and afterwards he graciously invited me to supper at his apartment – I was a nobody from the other side of the world, hoping for any crumbs of wisdom he might throw my way. Instantly, we had a great rapport, and I was completely in his thrall. The only fly in the ointment was that I wasn't very familiar with his body of work: only the snippets I had seen on YouTube of ballets such as *The Lady of the Camellias* and *A Midsummer Night's Dream*. The *Nijinsky* I had just watched was the first full-length ballet of his I'd seen on stage. While we were having an extremely warm and entertaining conversation, John asked me, 'Which of my ballets are you interested in?'

'Well,' I said, hoping I wasn't about to be exposed, 'I really like *Nijinsky.*' He began talking about *A Midsummer Night's Dream*, and offered to send me some DVDs of his works. I invited him to come out and see the company, as it's vital for choreographers to see a company to assess whether a particular piece would suit the dancers or not. During his summer break in 2002, he travelled to Melbourne to assess and watch the company. It took fourteen years, but in 2016 we performed *Nijinsky*.

It's never a quick process to court a world-famous choreographer in order to get them to give their work to a company they have not seen, but this one was particularly long because of a slight misunderstanding and my inexperience. John is very careful about his works and who he gives them to, so there was a period when I didn't hear from him and, assuming he had gone cool on the idea, I didn't pursue him. It turned out that was my mistake – he was waiting to hear from me about the next steps. The whole episode felt an awful lot like dating, and I ended up with the wrong end of the stick (also like dating). But with the help of Karen Kain, who was at the helm of The National Ballet of Canada and helped to smooth the way by sorting out my ineptitude, we ultimately locked in *Nijinsky*.

The entire trip gave me confidence and – importantly – contacts, while also reinforcing how much I would have to learn on the job. I knew I would be watched closely, as you would expect of the artistic head of one of the country's leading arts companies. There were people who thought mine was not a good appointment, that I was too inexperienced, that I'd never worked anywhere but Australia for any meaningful length of time, that I was a babe in the ballet woods. These were all legitimate concerns but, as always, I was determined to prove the doubters wrong.

I needed to lock in some big ballets, and I had the perfect opportunity rolling quickly towards me: the company's fortieth anniversary in 2002. One of the first phone calls I made when I was appointed artistic director was to Graeme Murphy, to see if he was interested in choreographing something new and grand for us – a kind of signature piece for the anniversary. Every major company milestone had featured one of his brilliant works: we staged his *Beyond Twelve* in our twenty-first birthday year, and his much-loved, very Australian *Nutcracker* was created to celebrate the thirtieth. In a corner of my memory, I had stored a conversation I had had with Graeme in 2000, when the company had revived this production. I asked him at the time, 'If you had the opportunity to re-create any of the other big classical ballets, which would it be?' He immediately answered: *Swan Lake*. While planning the fortieth anniversary program, this chat returned to me. As *Swan Lake* had been the first ballet the company had ever performed in 1962, I asked Graeme if he would consider creating a new production, and he agreed – it was a real 'Hooray!' moment. I spoke to him in August 2000 and the premiere was to be in September 2002, which is a punishingly short timeframe in which to bring a full-length ballet to fruition, especially as Graeme was also running Sydney Dance Company. But after some wrangling, he and designer Kristian Fredrikson were on board, and by September 2001 we were announcing the season.

I met with Graeme; his partner, Janet Vernon; and Kristian at Graeme and Janet's apartment in Sydney for the 'big idea' reveal. Graeme said he had two ideas: the first was something completely ridiculous about an owl that had a daughter who was a swan, and the swan must have been from Western Australia, because she was black. 'Okay,' I said calmly, 'we're not doing that one. What's version two?'

'Well, imagine,' Graeme said, that on the eve of her wedding, 'young Princess Odette discovers that her betrothed, Prince Siegfried, is having an affair with Baroness von Rothbart.'

Oh my god, I thought, *it's the Diana story!*

As the three of them kept talking and unravelling the layers of ideas that would go into this production, I realised I was completely smitten. They were clear that this was not a 'House of Windsor' drama, but simply a jumping-off point to tell a very well-known story in a new way. I knew that this was going to be a slightly precarious undertaking, but I also felt that it could be a real statement about my directorship and the artistic path ahead, and from that moment there was no looking back.

The decision to commission this ballet so early in my tenure seems riskier now than it did at the time – in my early days, I was so enthralled with everything (and blissfully ignorant in many ways) that it allowed me a certain amount of bluster. Still, there's no question that tinkering with a classic – no less than the most famous ballet in the world – is always a dangerous idea. Go too tame, and people are bored and disappointed. Go too radical, and people are angry. Piss people off too much, and subscriptions start to fall away. But if we got it right, audiences would fall in love with it. When I presented Graeme's *Swan Lake* to the board, I acknowledged this risk to them: this would either be one of the company's greatest successes, or my stint as artistic director would be the shortest in history.

Rehearsals began at the end of 2001, then picked up in intensity in July 2002, with opening night in Melbourne slated for September. The vibe in the studio was electric – the dancers knew they were working on something very special and there was a real energy in rehearsals. In June, The Royal Ballet came out on tour, bringing with them – of all things – their own *Swan Lake*. As I sat in the audience watching it, I thought, *This is beautiful, but what we are doing is equally compelling and very different.* The sets and design for our production were spectacular, and after a very tense production week, it debuted in mid-September with Simone Goldsmith as Odette and Steven Heathcote as Prince Siegfried. The evening was dreamlike – Simone was exquisite as Odette, the staging was perfect, the dancing sublime, and at the end of it the Melbourne audience got to its feet. I promoted Simone to principal at the afterparty that night, and the production quickly became the hottest ticket in town.

It was a huge relief that our big investment had paid off, and Graeme's genius had once again synchronised perfectly with our dancers' talents. Other parts of the job were far more challenging. Hardest of all was trying to get my head around managing people – something I had never done before and something that is not naturally part of my DNA. When I took on the job, I wanted to create a kind of ballet utopia, where everyone's dreams could come true. Of course, such a thing is entirely impossible: I had the hopes of seventy-two ambitious, talented young people resting on my shoulders, and inevitably I was going to have to disappoint some of them, and some would disappoint me. But it took me a long time to acknowledge that, even to myself.

I would have to learn how to lead, part of which was learning to be tougher than I wanted to be, or even than I felt. The first ballet we tackled under my directorship was *Giselle*, which was a blessing for me, having danced the same production just months earlier. Midway through the Melbourne season, I arrived home from the theatre one night, turned on the news and saw the footage of the September 11 terror attacks. Like many around the country, I stayed up for hours, watching in horror and trying to comprehend it all. The next day, all the dancers were quiet and a bit shell-shocked, so I called everyone together and said that the best way for us to go on in what seemed like a different world was to make our performances as compelling as we possibly could, to remind people watching us of the best aspects of humanity, and provide a few hours in the theatre in which they could leave the worries of the real world behind them and be transported. It was the first time I felt that my role as a leader was bigger than just making sure everyone danced well. It was also to gather and comfort, and provide everyone with a way forward when the path wasn't so clear.

I needed to recruit some more senior dancers – once again, the principal ranks were looking thin, especially among the males. When I finished dancing, there was only Steve and Matthew Trent left of the male principals, given the significant turnover when Ross left. On my trip overseas between dancing and directing, I had met with some ex–Australian Ballet dancers to see if I could bring them back into the fold. I talked to Nigel Burley and Rachel Rawlins, both of whom came back from The Royal Ballet in London, where they had been dancing, and also to Damien Welch and Kirsty Martin, who were at Nederlands Dans Theater and wanting to come home anyway, so the timing worked well. I also brought back Campbell McKenzie, who was working in the United Kingdom, and Margaret Illmann, who had been working in Europe, so I was pleased with the way the senior ranks were filling out with experienced artists. I also knew there were exceptionally talented dancers coming through the ranks, and I set about promoting some of them, including Robert Curran and Lucinda Dunn, whom I made principals at our 2002 launch.

Perhaps unsurprisingly, the split touring that we had locked ourselves into in order to secure more funding was causing headaches. In 2001, as Ross's last year became my first as director, we had two collaborations running simultaneously: about twenty dancers were doing *Tivoli* with Sydney Dance Company, and the rest were doing Stephen Baynes's *Requiem* and Natalie Weir's *Carmina Burana* in collaboration with the State Opera South Australia. It proved tricky, but we persevered because that was what the money was for. We split toured again in 2002 and 2003, when some dancers were involved in a new production of Meryl Tankard's *Wild Swans*. For this production, Meryl chose eighteen dancers she wanted to work with, which left the rest of the company free to prepare *Romeo and Juliet*. The *Wild Swans* process was difficult and I was too green in the job to manage the complexities of this production and the separation of the company's dancers for such a long period. On both 'teams' of dancers, there were many who found the rigours of effectively having two smaller companies working at the same time very stressful, and others who felt they had missed out on the opportunity to dance all the repertoire. Then at the end of it all, we had the problem of trying to put all the dancers back together again as one company – not as easy as it sounds, especially as they had been working as distinct units for such a long time. It was like separating a family for months and then expecting them all to instantly fall back into a cohesive whole.

Having, in essence, two companies had its advantages. It meant we could travel more widely than we had before and perform more shows away from Sydney and Melbourne, which we were acutely aware we needed to do. The company, after all, belongs to the whole country. Our company performs around 160 performances a year; adding more performances is a very big ask. Split touring gave us the opportunity to augment our regional touring arm – The Dancers Company, which at that time largely comprised senior students from the ballet school – by sending out smaller groups of the main company to larger centres such as Newcastle and Townsville. But the problem we hadn't factored in – and it proved to be the death knell in the end – was that when it came to doing the big, full-company productions that are the cornerstones of our repertoire, we simply didn't have enough rehearsal time with everyone together, and we were struggling to be ready to perform.

I was also careful to avoid splitting the company in any permanent or meaningful way – the last thing I wanted was to have an 'A' and 'B' company, where the 'B' group felt they were the weaker dancers. It was all repertoire-related, so that meant a dancer could be in the 'A' group for one production and the 'B' group for the next, depending on the choreographer's requirements. Meryl was very clear about whom she wanted for *Wild Swans*, but it left us very tight for numbers in *Romeo and Juliet* – if someone was injured or announced they were having a baby, we would have been somewhat screwed. Although neither of those eventualities happened at the time, I knew we couldn't ride our luck forever.

By 2004, it had become such a logistical nightmare – I felt we were flying by the seat of our pants – that we decided it would be the last year of split touring. It had taken its toll on the dancers, too, and there was generally much relief that it was coming to an end.

In the meantime, my honeymoon period had also drawn to a close, and the principal ranks that I had worked so hard to strengthen with gifted dancers were starting to crumble again. Some of the company's genuine stars came to tell me they were leaving. The most devastating of those was Simone Goldsmith, whom I adored and who had only recently been promoted to principal. Simone was the future of the company. But she was a perfectionist who drove herself hard, and in the end that had brought a level of anxiety that had taken the enjoyment out of dancing for her. Not long after that, Margaret Illmann told me she wanted to return to Europe, and then a chronic back problem Nigel Burley had been suffering reached the stage where he couldn't dance anymore, and he retired. That was three principals down. Then Nicole Rhodes left on exchange to the Royal Swedish Ballet to dance *The Sleeping Beauty*, fell in love, was offered a job there and then told me that she, too, was leaving to follow her heart. I tried to get her to divide her time between the companies, but she was adamant that she was going. Finally, Josh Consandine, whom I'd only recently promoted to principal, left to join Sydney Dance Company.

Just like that, a third of the principals left in quick succession. I started to have nightmares about press headlines saying 'Crisis at the ballet!' accompanying articles that would blame me for being a horrible director and declare that everyone at the company was unhappy. None of these screamers materialised, and the crisis was mostly in my head. We started 2004 positively, and a group of senior artists and soloists stepped up and performed principal roles – just as we had stepped up all those years ago when the 1981 strike created opportunities for young dancers in the company. Talented, ambitious people will always rise to the occasion.

We performed tribute programs to Sir Frederick Ashton and George Balanchine – who both would have turned 100 that year – the latter of which was called *Mr B*. Even though we were in a principal drought, the shows were fantastic, and the Balanchine people were very happy with the production. The whole experience taught me a lot about not catastrophising a situation, that there would always be a new generation of dancers. By this time, my rose-coloured glasses had come off and I had realised that in my new job I was not going to be able to make everyone's dreams come true (including my own on some occasions), but that I still had a job I adored leading a company that was my life.

Two key appointments had made my job much easier. Early on in my tenure, I knew I needed a music director. Music at The Australian Ballet had been treated in a fairly cavalier way since the 1970s, when the legendary John Lanchbery, the company's music director and chief conductor, had left to become music director with American Ballet Theatre. Many people had impressed on me the need for that to change, and for us to treat music with the seriousness it deserved if we wanted to be a world-class ballet company. Ross had taken early steps to bring American Ballet Theatre's resident conductor Charles Barker out to join us, but ultimately he went to join The Royal Ballet with Ross.

My idea was to have a kind of 'year of discovery' in 2002, in which I invited a string of conductors to spend time with us as guests over the course of the year, in the hope of finding the right match for a permanent role. Ted Branson, who was artistic director with the West Australian Ballet, suggested that we invite Nicolette Fraillon as one of those guests – he had worked with her in the Netherlands and Perth and had been very impressed. From the first day Nicolette joined us as a guest, I knew she would be the one to lead us in all things musical, and her appointment was one of the most influential and successful I made in my time as director.

As a colleague and a friend, Nicolette always encouraged me to be bold with my ideas and believe in them, and she always had my back in tough times. Nicolette taught me a great deal, not only about music, but about managing people and the power of educating through entertainment. So much of what I have achieved as director was only possible with her by my side as music director.

The other significant appointment that happened early in my tenure was Richard Evans, who joined the company in 2002 as the new executive director. Ian McRae, who had been so supportive and kind, was instrumental in guiding me through those early months, when I was unsure and hugely inexperienced. He was the perfect mentor, never saying an outright 'no' to crazy ideas, but gently pointing out the potential pitfalls before I tumbled into them. He was always available to offer wise counsel when I was struggling, or being too ambitious, enthusiastic or naive. I was devastated when he told me he was leaving, which I dealt with in my characteristic way: *Maybe he won't*, I told myself. *Maybe he'll change his mind.* He didn't, of course, and while his departure was a wrench, he managed it in such a way that it was as painless as possible.

I was lucky enough to be a part of the selection process for Ian's replacement – as, in effect, the company's joint CEOs, the executive director and I needed to be able to work together clearly, collaboratively and dynamically for the sake of the company. Richard Evans was the man we decided on. At his first interview I was a bit put off by his confidence, but by the second interview, I had completely changed my mind, and announced I was 'in love' to anyone who cared to hear it. We worked brilliantly together for the five years Richard held the job. He was a radical departure from the wise father-figure of Ian: he came into the company like a tornado, full of energy and enthusiasm and exuding the feeling – no doubt believing it, too – that anything was possible. In many ways, he was like one of those boys at school who were the polar opposite of me (and whom I wished I had been): naughty, popular, outgoing and friends with everyone. He could walk into a room and everyone would want to hang out with him.

Richard, Nicolette, Patrick McIntyre – who was appointed marketing director – and I became the ballet's 'brains trust', and we had a ridiculous amount of fun together. It was a time of change in the way arts companies were being run (and marketed, for that matter – the technological revolution was really taking hold), and we were ready to embrace new ways of thinking and learning. Nicolette was full of brilliant ideas, and Richard wanted to make them happen: his mantra was 'Don't think about the money'. 'Don't just give me the things you think we can afford,' he would say. 'I want your biggest ideas so we can make them happen.' We took the company through a major rebranding exercise, bolstering the website, working with a design team and taking fresh, vital photographs of the dancers to use in our season brochures, on our website and on social media. Suddenly, the ballet company was no longer looking strict and neat, but rather young, sexy and dynamic – as it was.

One of the most important jobs an artistic director has to do is the programming, and in a flagship company like The Australian Ballet, the trick is to strike a balance between the traditional story ballets that audiences – particularly the older members who are a key demographic – like to see, and fresh new works that are risky but challenging, and that progress the art form. Choreographers with international reputations are in high demand around the world, and often a ballet has to be commissioned several years before it actually comes to fruition. One of my important, and challenging, tasks was to identify choreographers who were on their way up, as well as entice the established ones to work with our company.

When I was on exchange with The National Ballet of Canada as a dancer, I met Assis Carreiro, who was in charge of the company's education and publication programs. She later left Canada and became the artistic director of DanceEast in Ipswich in the United Kingdom. While working there, she had the brilliant idea of bringing artistic directors from around the world together for a 'rural retreat' to share ideas and issues, and discuss the future of dance. She invited me to the first one in 2003, and I was chuffed to be there among some of the biggest names in world dance. One of the knottiest problems we discussed was that there were fewer and fewer choreographers around the world creating new works using traditional classical technique – most of the dynamism was around a more contemporary approach to dance-making. We talked about ways to nurture young or inexperienced choreographers and give them opportunities to create new works. I mulled this over and when I returned to Australia, we came up with the idea of *bodytorque* – a permanent fixture on the calendar that was set aside specifically to allow young choreographers the chance to make works for a professional dance company before a big audience. The Australian Ballet had always had a choreographic program, but it had been run in a rather ad hoc fashion and only really given an airing when there was some spare time in the program – which was hardly ever. Even though we missed a few years of *bodytorque* in the lead-up to the fiftieth anniversary festivities, it remains one of my proudest achievements, and through it we have nurtured several brilliant new choreographers, including Alice Topp, Tim Harbour and Lucas Jervies. All three have gone on to work on mainstage productions after beginning with *bodytorque*, and I'm convinced there will be more to come.

Slowly, I was lining up a strong array of established international choreographers to work with the company, too. I had been lucky enough to have British choreographer Christopher Wheeldon stage his ballet *Mercurial Manoeuvres* in 2002, and I had Wayne McGregor and Alexei Ratmansky signed up to create works for us as part of our long Ballets Russes tribute. It was particularly important that I had Australian dance-makers to create peculiarly Australian works, too, so Stephen Page from Bangarra Dance Theatre and our resident choreographers Stephen Baynes and Stanton Welch also created ballets for us.

It was Nicolette who had the idea of celebrating our extraordinary dance history with a tribute to the Ballets Russes. This was the touring dance company led by the famous impresario Sergei Diaghilev in the early 20th century, which created a whole new form of modern ballet. After Diaghilev's death, Wassily de Basil formed a new company, Les Ballets Russes de Monte Carlo, which revived a lot of Diaghilev's works and created a sensation when it toured Australia in the late 1930s. One of the dancers on the 1938 tour, Edouard Borovansky, decided to stay in Australia after the tour, where he later founded the Borovansky Ballet, which was the precursor to The Australian Ballet. The Ballets Russes were hugely important to the spread and popularity of modern ballet throughout the world, and Australia was key to that. It was a rich part of our cultural history that was largely unrecognised: we agreed it needed to be explored and celebrated.

We decided to present a combination of 'tribute' works from that time and commission new ballets to reimagine some of that repertoire. Nicolette had obtained some Australian Research Council (ARC) grants during her time as head of the Australian National University's school of music, so we underpinned these revivals with some research undertaken thanks to another ARC grant in conjunction with the National Library of Australia and Adelaide University. That collaboration became a four-year project. We were lucky to have some of the Ballets Russes's dancers living in Australia and they joined us to stage some of these works. This included Irina Baronova, one of the three famous so-called baby ballerinas who shot to fame as young teenagers, alongside her fellow dancers from that time Anna Volkova, Tatiana Leskova and Valerie Tweedie. It was extraordinary for our dancers to work on these ballets with access to their knowledge and expertise. Their participation provided a link back to their performances and an authenticity of style and spirit that is often missing when reproducing these works. It was fascinating hearing them talk about those early Ballets Russes tours and working with the company's star choreographer, Mikhail Fokine (which was not easy, by all accounts). Ballet is an art form that is handed down through generations of dancers, and this was made all the more poignant and timely as many of these dear women were not with us by the time we completed this project.

As we were busy planning all of this, I received an unexpected surprise: in 2004, I was made a Member of the Order of Australia (AM). It was a total shock and a great thrill – I still have no idea who nominated me. Steve Heathcote and Christine Walsh had received honours while they were still dancing, so I assumed my time had passed. But out of the blue, I received a letter asking if I would accept the honour, and I was extremely humbled by it. It was particularly satisfying that I could share this honour with my dad, who had stood up for and by me all those years ago when I was a kid determined to learn ballet. I knew Mum would have been proud, too, especially after she counselled me through the tough school days, dispensing wise advice from the other side of her steaming ironing board. It's a nice feeling to do something that makes your family proud, even when you are in your forties.

There were, however, more challenges on the horizon, including the problem of touring the company internationally. In 2002, we were planning to undertake our first major overseas tour during my directorship. The company was scheduled to travel to China in 2003 when the SARS virus hit. The epidemic was so severe and travelling so rapidly that we had no choice but to cancel the tour, as neither the dancers nor the sponsors would have had much appetite for it. In 2004, we planned to travel to the United States, a trip partly funded by the Australian government and the Kennedy Center in Washington. This trip, too, was abandoned – this time because the government money dried up. There was a change of leadership at the Kennedy Center that meant the planned 'Australian festival' was cancelled. In the end it was probably just as well, as they had allocated us only the smaller Eisenhower Theater at the centre that would have struggled to accommodate the Murphy *Swan Lake*.

We then planned to tour the United Kingdom in 2005, and given all the strife we'd had with the other aborted tours, this was a huge deal. We were scheduled to first go to Cardiff, to the new Millennium Centre, then to London and the Coliseum theatre, where we'd had such success dancing for Princess Diana all those years ago. We were taking Murphy's *Swan Lake*, so it was a massive undertaking, and there was great excitement about it in the company.

The night before we left was the opening night of Sydney Dance Company's Melbourne season of *Grand*. At the party afterwards, Richard Evans received news on his phone about the London bombings, a series of coordinated attacks on the city's transport network. Fifty-two people had been killed and many more injured. The next morning, we met to discuss whether the tour should go ahead and decided that as our first stop was Cardiff for a week, things in London would have settled down by the time we got there. We boarded the plane with noticeably heightened security at the airport.

The Cardiff season went extremely well and a lot of the London press came to see it, which helped to sell the remaining shows. The next week, we arrived safely in London and John Howard, the Australian prime minister, was in the audience on opening night. The following day, we had two shows, and during the matinee a second series of attempted bomb attacks took place. Thankfully, all the dancers were safe inside the theatre, but it was incredibly frightening nonetheless, and devastating for our London friends and the city. It meant that audiences became nervous about going out, so our ticket sales suffered as a consequence for the remainder of the season. The silver lining from this came the following January, when the company was awarded the London Critics' Circle Award for best foreign company. It was also the tour that fully showcased Murphy's *Swan Lake* and triggered worldwide interest in staging the ballet, which continues to this day.

By this time in my directorship, I had settled into the role with reasonable comfort. I had (reluctantly) accepted that I wasn't going to be able to please everyone, and had become better – though still not great – at having difficult discussions with dancers. I had sunk myself into my work using the borderline-religious zeal with which I approached everything to do with ballet. And despite the difficulties and challenges, I was loving every minute of it.

As usual, my personal life was relegated to the backburner. I was seeing some men, but on the quiet and deliberately with no strings attached. Then, late in 2004, I met up with my friend Margaret Bourke at a Melbourne Theatre Company (MTC) open day. Margaret had taken on the role of production manager at the Melbourne Theatre Company, which at the time was staging *The Sapphires* under the directorship of a brilliant Indigenous director named Wesley Enoch. Margaret introduced us, but I was fairly distracted, mostly because I was hungry and anxious to go out to dinner.

I thought nothing more of our meeting, but a few years later, thanks to another mutual friend with an eye for a match, Wesley and I would meet again, and before long Mr Enoch would take centre stage in my life.

CHAPTER 9

Coming out, and moving on

It was Richard Evans who outed me, firstly to myself. In 2002, when Richard started as executive director, we were having a 'getting to know you' chat over coffee. 'So,' he said matter-of-factly, 'you're gay?' I hesitated. I'd never been asked that question so bluntly before – I was still thinking of myself as something of an enigma in terms of my private life. 'Yes,' I replied. Finally, I had admitted it to myself, as well as to a friend and colleague. It felt wonderfully freeing to be open like this and to be seen as who I was by someone who wasn't judging, just curious.

Having said that, it changed very little in my life. In 1996, during Maina's last year as artistic director, and after I realised I was never going to be totally happy in a relationship with a woman (nor be totally committed), I started to explore my sexuality with other men. I had heard there were phone lines you could ring to meet gay men, which was an exhilarating and scary prospect – I decided to jump in and give it a go. I knew I needed, as Kelvin had told me all those years ago, to sort myself out. I liked the idea of the anonymity of the phone lines and, always a little shy in social situations, I was relieved to not have to be sitting on a bar stool talking to someone who'd had a few too many. The whole experience, predictably enough, was a bit of a lucky dip. I'd call the number, be hooked up with someone, we'd chat, and if we liked each other, we'd meet up. It was largely anonymous and with no strings attached, which was very appealing to me at the time as I was not ready to fully commit to a relationship. I felt like I was on a voyage of discovery about my sexuality. I also enjoyed having another life, away from the company, that I didn't have to share with anyone. It was my little secret. This continued over the years, and when I became director there were a couple of special men in my life, but we operated on the understanding that what we had was not a relationship. This suited everyone just fine, and falling in love never really entered my head – I was utterly obsessed with my job, and any time beyond that I spent with my friends.

That all changed when I met Wesley again. After the brief introduction by Margaret at the MTC open day, she and I went off for dinner and that was that. The next connection was early in 2007, during one of the company's seasons in Brisbane, when I stayed, as I always did, with my friend Sue Street, a professor in the arts at Queensland University of Technology (QUT) whom I had met through my friend Nerida O'Loughlin. Sue had taught Wesley when he was a student at QUT, and they had kept in touch. One night while I was there, Sue invited Wesley over for a drink.

Wesley was born to a Noonuccal Nuugi father and a white mother on Stradbroke Island in Queensland, the second of four children and the eldest boy. His parents were hard workers who raised their children to be strong, thoughtful and caring people. The family later moved to Brisbane, where Wesley, a very bright child, showed a particular aptitude for English. Like me, he had found his 'voice' as a young boy through performance, drawn as he was to the theatre. He later studied at Queensland University of Technology, where Sue had been his ballet teacher. He went on to become one of the country's leading theatre directors and playwrights.

Now here he was sitting across the table from me, intelligent, thoughtful, handsome and – that thing that always produced a high level of anxiety in me – very cool. It was a hugely enjoyable night, and I revelled in the stimulating conversation between Sue and Wesley – he was a fascinating man and I felt a bit guilty I hadn't been friendlier at our first meeting. After he left, Sue asked, 'Isn't Wesley *lovely*?' and the penny dropped – she was setting us up. 'Yes,' I said, 'he is really charming, but way too sophisticated for me!' Why would such a star of the arts scene be interested in a former ballet dancer? When it came to dating and relationships, I was still that nervous little kid wandering around the oval looking for someone to play with, and wondering if I was about to be pushed into the dirt.

I didn't see Wesley again for a while after that and put him to the back of my mind. Then in April 2008, the new prime minister, Kevin Rudd, held his 2020 Summit in Canberra, which brought together a thousand Australians from a wide range of fields to imagine what the country might look like in 2020. I was lucky enough to be chosen as one of the representatives after a complex and highly competitive nomination process, and I was placed in the Towards a Creative Australia stream. There I found myself among luminaries such as Cate Blanchett and Joel Edgerton, as well as writers, designers, directors and a host of other creative people. At first, I felt shy and out of place – once again, I was trying to keep my dagginess to a minimum, waiting to be shunned. But that didn't happen, and over the course of the two-day summit I kept finding myself in groups with Wesley, where I was very grateful for a familiar face. He was at the centre of a lot of the debates, with big ideas and opinions that always garnered respect. I chatted with Wesley and several others between sessions, and even though I came away not sure exactly what it achieved, I had nonetheless thoroughly enjoyed all the conversations and ideas, and I returned to Melbourne energised about my own job and the future of the ballet company.

After the summit, we were all able to keep in touch via email groups, so the conversations and exchange of ideas that had begun in Canberra continued. One group email invited us to go on an archaeological dig in central Australia, where there had been some great discoveries of prehistoric fossils. Shortly after I read it, my inbox dinged again; this time it was an email from Wesley, asking if I was going on the dig. I replied that I wasn't, as there was always so much ballet business to attend to. I did notice, though, that this wasn't the usual 'reply all' email, but one just to me. This started a chat back and forth between the two of us, leading to a promise to 'catch up sometime'.

I was really enjoying getting to know Wesley a little better, even if only by email – it was exciting to get off 'Ballet Island' for a while and learn about him and his work. Both of us had jobs that involved a lot of travel, so it was hard to meet up, but a couple of weeks later we were in Melbourne at the same time, so we arranged to meet for coffee. This turned out to be something of a misnomer, as neither of us drinks coffee, but we did have a grand time over peppermint tea in a little cafe near the Block Arcade. I really valued time with a new, non-ballet friend, and again we promised to keep in touch.

A few weeks passed and then we found we were both in Sydney, so we arranged to meet up for dinner in Surrey Hills, where Wesley was staying. I was leaving the Opera House to meet him – unusually, I was not staying for the performance – when Richard Evans, who had since left The Australian Ballet to become chief executive of the Opera House, noticed me going and called to me in jest: 'Where are you off to? Is there another show on?' I explained that I was having dinner with Wesley Enoch. 'Oh, so you're going on a date!' he replied. 'No,' I replied, explaining that we had met at the 2020 Summit and kept in touch, which I genuinely meant – as far as I knew, Wesley and I were just friends. When I met Wesley at dinner, I relayed my earlier conversation with Richard, thinking Wesley would get a laugh from the idea of us dating. 'Well, yes,' Wesley said seriously, 'this is a date.' Once again, I had had no idea what was going on, but this placed the evening in a whole new light that delighted and terrified me. The cool guy likes me! At the end of the dinner, our parting embrace was a long one, and as we walked off in opposite directions we caught each other looking back. It was just like a rom-com moment, and there was definitely romance in the air.

I was 'dating' Wesley! This changed everything. I was working on my fitness at the time, and this new relationship status made me bump it up a notch so that I was 'match fit' for when the dating turned to full-blown romance. The gym was working a treat – I hadn't been in such good shape since I stopped dancing. Our phone calls became more frequent and more intimate, and my heart started to flutter a little whenever I saw his name come up on the screen. Our busy schedules and travel continued to make it difficult to see each other in person as often as we liked, but we were becoming closer and learning more about each other, and revelling in those heady days of a new relationship. I was ready to take the next step with Wesley, but he was being gallantly coy – he wanted to make sure, he told me, that this relationship was for the long haul. 'In the meantime,' he wisely said, 'we'll never get this time back, these early days when we're getting to know each other, let's just make the most of every moment.' It was the first time in my life that anyone had told me they wanted to grow old with me. This one was a keeper.

We started doing all the little things that you do for each other when you're enamoured, things I had somehow missed out on along the way. Wesley played me a song that he said reminded him of me – Jamie Lidell's 'Another Day' – and then bought me the album on a CD as I was such a Luddite that I still used CDs. He then bought me an iPod Shuffle and I made a playlist of songs for us to listen to when we were not together. It was really teenaged, schmaltzy stuff, but at forty-five I guessed I might never experience that feeling of 'young love' again, and it was intoxicating – what added such lustre to these emotions was finally gaining acceptance of myself and the happiness I felt in my own skin. By this stage, I was ready for us to consummate our relationship, but Wesley wanted to wait and savour our celibate time, so we could concentrate on learning about each other with no distractions. This almost drove me crazy, but on the upside, I was putting a tremendous amount of energy into my gym program.

In August 2008, we went to the Australian Dance Awards together at Arts Centre Melbourne. We left together and as we went to go our separate ways home, we stood on the corner of Swanston and Bourke streets, the number 96 tram rattling in the distance, and we kissed. Not just a peck on the cheek, but a proper, romantic kiss. It was, again, just like a movie, with the camera spinning around us (fireworks? Butterflies at the very least) – I never wanted it to end. Luckily, the city was pretty deserted at that time, as pashing in public is not really my thing. But I was elated and, by this stage, falling deeply in love. I still think of that night every time I pass that corner of Melbourne, and the night has become our anniversary. Not long after that, when we had been dating for about six months, we finally became lovers in every sense of the word. I was blissfully happy; everything about Wesley fuelled my senses – his humour, intelligence, passion and generosity. We were now in that heady place of actually being a couple and referring to each other as 'my boyfriend'.

Wesley was still travelling a lot with his work, and these separations became harder and more obvious to us. We had an unwritten rule that when we were travelling internationally, we wouldn't call each other, mostly because of time differences and the general logistics. It is a rule we still adhere to. The first time I felt tested by it, though, was when Wesley headed an Australian delegation to Samoa for a First Nations arts festival and was gone for a couple of weeks. I am pretty pragmatic and found plenty to occupy myself with for the duration, but I missed him terribly, and took to writing my thoughts in a diary. It is lovely to look back on it now and relive the first blush of our relationship.

In October 2008, the company was travelling to Paris and I decided to ask Wesley to come with me. I had always wanted to be in Paris and in love, and this was my big chance. He was a little hesitant at first as he was a freelance director at the time, and being away for an extended period might mean missing opportunities. He was also not sure about me paying for it, as he is fiercely independent. But I eventually sold him on it by explaining it was a gift to me to make a dream come true.

For the company and me as artistic director, there was a lot riding on this tour. The Australian Ballet hadn't performed in Paris since 1965 and the company, still in its infancy, won an award for Peggy van Praagh's production of *Giselle*. It was important that we acquitted ourselves well. We were scheduled to dance at the Théâtre du Châtelet, where Diaghilev's Ballets Russes had first performed in 1909. We were in the last years of our Ballets Russes project and we presented two programs to the French audiences: the first was Stephen Page's *Rites*, performed with Bangarra Dance Theatre, alongside Krzysztof Pastor's *Symphonie Fantastique*; the second was Murphy's *Swan Lake*. The double bill was received very well, with the audience beguiled and surprised by *Rites*. *Swan Lake* was also a great success, with *Le Figaro* newspaper heading their review with 'The Australians Put Fire Back into Swan Lake'.

Wesley already knew Paris well, having spent several months there in 2002 on an Australia Council residency – it was there that he began writing his play *The Story of the Miracles at Cookie's Table*. It was glorious having him there with the company's dancers and watching them all interact. It was the first time Wesley had spent a lengthy amount of time with the dancers and the first major integration of my personal relationship into my work life. After the first few days of interest and curiosity from the dancers, it became normal very quickly. International touring is a good way to start or introduce new relationships, given that we're all forced to spend large amounts of time together every day.

We made time for fun, too. On a free day, Wesley and I went to the Musée du Quai Branly, which was on both our bucket lists, because of the sublime collection of First Nations art. On our way there, I was scammed by a man who claimed he had found a ring and couldn't locate its owner, so he wanted to sell it to me for 10 euros. He was very insistent and I was keen to get rid of him, so I handed over the money. Wesley was a bit annoyed at me for caving in to such an obvious con, but I liked the idea of the ring being a memento of our time in Paris, in love! I kept it in my suitcase and gave it to Wesley as part of his Christmas present at the end of the year – he still has it, a band of copper in a lovely shade of green.

Another delight of this trip was that Liz came to visit with her eldest son and my godson, Jack. It gave me a huge amount of joy to introduce Wesley and Liz to each other and see two extremely important people in my life hit it off instantly. I also enjoyed spending time with Jack, who was growing into a lovely young man. After Paris, Wesley headed home to Australia while the company and I went on to London and Manchester. I'll never forget this magical period that brought together all of my great loves at one time.

By the end of 2008, with our relationship going strong, I knew it was time to tell my family about Wesley. Through all those years of trying to work out and come to terms with my sexuality, I made a promise to myself that when I met someone really special, I would tell them. Wesley was that person. On a trip home to Perth just after Christmas, I first shared my news with the person to whom I always told my secrets: my sister, Di. While we had always been extremely close – as kids we used to try to find out what our parents were getting the other one for Christmas and birthdays, and then report back – there were some things we never talked about, and one of those was my love life. Given it was a long time since my last 'girlfriend' and knowing me as she did, I think Di expected that if I was introducing a long-term partner, it was likely to be a man. When I told her about Wesley, she was delighted, as I knew she would be.

For some reason, I hesitated to tell Dad. It was a strange response, because had she been alive, telling Mum would have been far harder than telling Dad – she always worried a lot about what other people thought, a trait I have inherited, often to my detriment. If I had ever been in trouble of any kind, Dad would have been the one I called. But I kept putting off breaking the news, waiting for the right moment, or perhaps just giving myself time to muster my courage. On the last night of my stay before heading home to start the 2009 year, I knew I had to tell Dad about Wesley and, at forty-six, come out to him. Just before I went to bed, I said, 'Dad, there is something I have to tell you. I've met someone.'

'That's great,' he replied, and before he could say anything else, I interrupted with: 'He is a man and his name is Wesley.' My dad looked at me and said: 'I'm so happy for you, son; it's so important to have someone in your life.' At that moment, I couldn't have loved my father more, and as was so often the case, I realised I had been worrying about nothing. He was instantly accepting and wanted to know more about Wesley, so we stayed up talking and I told Dad about Wesley's career and his heritage. Dad was truly thrilled, and immediately wanted to meet Wesley. It's strange, as a middle-aged person, to still be craving your parent's approval, but his unquestioning support meant the world to me, and it still does. In the years since that conversation, Wesley has become part of our family and Dad is as proud of his achievements as he is of mine. He always calls to tell me he's seen Wesley on the television and how brilliantly he expressed his views.

With that out of the way, there was only one more obvious step in our relationship – moving in together. We both had a place to live in Melbourne, but neither was right for the two of us, so we decided to find a place that was new and, as it were, 'neutral' territory.

We were in luck. Through a friend of Wesley's we found the perfect place in Collingwood, with two bedrooms and an open-plan kitchen and dining area for entertaining. A beautiful balcony upstairs gave magical views of the Melbourne skyline. Bliss! We often had people over for dinner and we found we shared a house well. Wesley was still travelling a lot for work so I often had the place to myself, which I enjoyed, having lived alone for more than ten years. Wesley also revelled in the times when I was touring and he had the place to himself, so we fell into a very comfortable rhythm.

Towards the end of 2010, Wesley had the chance to move to Brisbane to take up the post of artistic director of the Queensland Theatre Company, so our time in Collingwood came to an end. This was particularly difficult as Wesley was moving on (and so far away!) to a prestigious new job, while I was returning to my little apartment in the city and losing our shared life. I was elated for him, though, and while long-distance relationships can be tricky, I knew that we were both used to it and that we'd be able to manage without any problems. We made a rule, then and there, that we would never go for longer than three weeks without seeing each other, a rule we have consistently broken, and still do. However, I cheered myself up a little with a bathroom renovation in my flat, which made returning to a largely solo life more agreeable.

While everything was travelling smoothly in my relationship, I was struggling with managing people at work. It astonished me that I continued to find it hard – I had thought, when I took on the job, that managing people would be easy, as I loved all the dancers and had been a dancer myself. Conversely, I thought talking about budgets, financing and scheduling would be a nightmare, but actually I enjoyed it more than I expected (and understood it better than I anticipated, too). Maina once told me that directing The Australian Ballet was 'like driving a Rolls-Royce', and I came to know what she meant. It's a very well-oiled machine, with experts on every aspect of the company's operations. I learnt to roll with the punches. Sometimes programming fell through, but there was always an alternative. Though I developed a better handle on it, budgeting remained a bit of a dark art to me: sometimes we seemed to have plenty of money, while other times it seemed incredibly tight, and I was not always sure exactly why that was. But managing the dancers' expectations was fraught. I remember very early on in my tenure coming out of my first principal salary negotiation completely shell-shocked. 'What is this?' I asked Ian McRae at the time. 'Are they always like this?'

'Oh yes,' he replied.

When I was a dancer, I had no idea about any of that. I'd go in, they'd say: we'd like to offer this amount of money, and I'd say: thank you very much. I never asked for more, or even realised it was an option.

The dancers' salaries are fixed through an enterprise bargaining arrangement, and the higher the rank, the higher the salary. But the principals' salaries are negotiated every year and fluctuate largely based on workload as well as performance. Those who have had long periods off due to injury or pregnancy are not usually in line for big pay rises, as their performing is curtailed. But I was blown away by the strength of the dancers' advocacy on pay. I also quickly came to the (somewhat painful) realisation that I was not going to be able to provide 'ballet nirvana' for everyone, and that I would have to live with their disappointment and, on occasion, anger. I've vastly improved at managing people over the years, but I still struggle. Every year, I have to tell people that I will not be promoting them, or that there is no longer a place for them in the company. Sometimes they know it's time to go and accept it graciously; other times they are bitterly disappointed or hurt.

Like all workplaces, we have annual performance reviews. They are laborious processes, requiring me, with the input of the ballet staff, to write reports for each of our seventy-seven dancers. I usually have several sleepless nights in the lead-up to the one-on-one meetings to discuss each dancer's performance and future. One of the consistent pieces of feedback the dancers have given me over the years is that they find me too optimistic and bullish in these interviews – misleadingly so. For example, I may have told them that everything was going fabulously and that they were right on track, which they read as 'one day you will be a principal', but what I was really saying was that they were doing everything they should for the rank they held. I can see, though, how they might have thought I was promising something I wasn't – it was that old tendency of mine to be a bit of a Pollyanna. And I remember how hard it was, sometimes, to read artistic directors when I was a dancer, so I'd made a conscious effort to be more forthright and realistic in these conversations. I also knew that I might be wrong – I never forgot that Maina had told me I'd never be a prince, yet eventually I was. These things are largely a matter of opinion and can seem wildly unjust to the dancers, but I need to make decisions that I think are in the best interests of the company as a whole.

Fortunately, I don't have to do this entirely on my own. I always have the artistic associate and principal ballet mistress Fiona Tonkin with me, who has been a godsend since she joined the teaching staff in 2003. I have rarely met someone in the ballet sphere with more integrity, nor a greater capacity for hard work – she spends more hours in the studio than anyone in the building. She is my go-to person when I want to take the temperature of the company, or when I need advice about a particular dancer. It turned out that the great rapport we shared when we danced together transferred easily and naturally to life after dancing. Fiona and Danny Radojevic, when he was my associate director, have been the most steadfast and wise colleagues, especially when times were tough. Fortuitously, Steven Heathcote joined the teaching staff after Danny left in 2014, and it was a pleasure to have him back as part of the team.

At the start of every year, Fiona and I meet with the new dancers as a group, and many times I have heard her tell them they will get out of their ballet careers what they put in. This is wise advice, and to me the capacity to learn and consistently work hard is the greatest measure of success. I have seen dancers who were worthy members in the corps de ballet grow and shine through sheer hard work and determination; conversely, I've seen extremely talented dancers waste their natural abilities. These are the most frustrating dancers – the ones blessed with natural ability but who coast and have probably never pushed themselves in anything because it has always come so easily to them. These dancers often look to shift the blame for their flat or disappointing performances – the floor was sticky/slippery/hard, the costume was too tight, the music was too fast/slow or both – but it invariably comes back to their dedication to the art form and preparedness to work hard to be the best dancer they possibly can be.

In 2007, to my great disappointment, Richard Evans, who by that stage was a great friend as well as colleague, left the ballet to run the Sydney Opera House. Richard's replacement was Valerie Wilder, the first woman to be executive director of The Australian Ballet. I had met Valerie when I was a dancer on exchange with The National Ballet of Canada in 1989, where she was joint artistic director. Valerie had been both a dancer and artistic director with The National Ballet, after which she became executive director before moving to the same role with the Boston Ballet. She brought huge experience to the role with us and, over the years she held the post, her great legacy was a focus on philanthropy. She and the company's philanthropy director, Kenneth Watkins, established an extraordinarily secure financial base for the company by creating a philanthropic framework which has facilitated the building of a large endowment that will support the company into the future. Valerie realised from the start that the gap between costs and revenue was growing, and philanthropy was the obvious way to bridge that.

By 2010, heading into my tenth anniversary as artistic director, I hit a bit of a slump. We had survived the global financial crisis, but it meant there was less money to go around, and that in turn had a significant impact on programming and creativity. The process leading up to the 2012 program – the fiftieth anniversary – was fraught and I was completely wrung out. It wasn't the first trying time of my directorship, but it was a particularly exhausting one. We had also come through a difficult renewal for the 2006 season, when subscriptions had taken a dive and audiences were unsure of what to expect in the first year of the Ballets Russes celebration. As the year progressed, it played out much better than expected, but we put in place the plan to stage Peter Wright's *The Nutcracker* in 2007, which steadied the ship for the subscriptions campaign (it was a triumphant success on stage, too).

After these challenges of the preceding few years, I found my attitude at the beginning of 2010 was different, and my mood dark. Wesley was telling me to leave. 'Why are you still there?' he would ask. I knew I had more to do and I wanted to stay; the idea of leading the company through its fiftieth anniversary was an enticing one. I was also very aware that it would be all-consuming and I needed to get into a better headspace. The board's chair, Chris Knoblanche, suggested I take a few extra weeks of leave over the summer break, to clear my mind and relax before coming back to tackle 2011. I was already planning to go to another 'rural retreat' with other artistic directors in Ipswich in the United Kingdom, so this seemed a great idea – I took another week or so of pure holiday, which I dubbed my 'grumpy leave'. I think after almost ten years of the relentless pace, I was a little burnt out and Chris, in his wisdom, saw that I needed to let off a bit of steam. I went to Rome and had a magnificent, relaxing time. It helped a lot and I returned to work refreshed and ready to take on anything.

The fiftieth anniversary was a monolith. It was wildly ambitious, with a three-year build-up to it and festivities of every imaginable kind almost every day in 2012. There were documentaries, intense media interest, a set of stamps, a glorious coffee-table book tribute called *Luminous*, a crazy tour of New York for a week…on and on it went. The dance program was also huge. We had new works commissioned, including one from Graeme Murphy called *The Narrative of Nothing*, with a commissioned score by Brett Dean. Gideon Obarzanek created a work called *There's Definitely a Prince Involved*, a deconstruction of *Swan Lake* that involved four of his Chunky Move dancers along with others from our company, a bit of a romp that upset a lot of our subscribers. The program finished with a collaboration with Bangarra Dance Theatre, with Stephen Page choregraphing *Warumuk – in the dark night*, the first ballet he had made for us based on First Nations stories. We also revived John Cranko's *Onegin*, which had been out of the repertoire for many years and which I was excited to bring back. And we designed a program that celebrated our history, in which we revived Sir Robert Helpmann's *The Display*, the first original Australian work the company produced, and combined it with Glen Tetley's contemporary work *Gemini* and Murphy's *Beyond Twelve*. Stephen Baynes created a new *Swan Lake* with designer Hugh Colman, and we invited dance companies from around the country to be part of the *Let's Dance* program, which included Tim Harbour's commissioned work *Sweedeedee*, featuring the now-retired Justine Summers and her former dance partner Steven Heathcote alongside his daughter, Mia. It was a stunning, huge undertaking.

And it went on and on. We did our exhausting, whirlwind tour of New York, then came back and went straight into the *Onegin* season in Melbourne – in hindsight, complete madness. We finished with a gala program in October, for which we invited dancers from around the world, while the company performed Harald Lander's showstopping *Études*. I also took my first foray into choreography, creating a curtain-raiser for the show called *Overture*. Landing myself with this was another moment of lunacy, as I'd never choreographed anything more than extended exercises in class. In the lead-up to the gala, several guest artists pulled out for various reasons and there was a crazy scramble to replace them. I felt like I'd given myself an impossible task by adding choreography to my load – it would never be ready in time. Despite this fear, it gave me huge fulfilment being in the studio making the ballet, and in the best theatrical tradition it mercifully all came together on the night. It was, though, a lesson in taking on too much, which I'd like to say I learnt, but unfortunately it was a mistake I was doomed to repeat.

At the end of all of this, as we started the annual summer break, I boarded a Qantas flight from Sydney to Melbourne that was playing a series of mini-documentaries we had made to celebrate our big birthday. As I sat there watching it, the anniversary finally over, I burst into floods of exhausted tears. The whole experience had been very worthwhile, but I'm convinced it shaved a few years off my life.

The following year, in 2013, Valerie Wilder announced she was leaving the company, and the search for her replacement proved difficult. I was, as always, on the selection panel, but I don't think we had developed a coherent and unified idea of exactly what we were looking for in the next executive director. There was a lot of talk about getting a 'disruptor' – someone from outside the sector who might examine things with fresh eyes. I was very wary of this and stamped my foot a bit about candidates I felt were not suitable. The field was re-examined and Libby Christie was appointed. She was the perfect person for the role, with experience in the corporate world and the arts, and possessing great energy and dynamism. These past eight years of partnership with Libby have seen the company thrive, and so many huge projects have been achieved: increasing the number of dancers; refurbishing and extending our home base, The Primrose Potter Australian Ballet Centre; and putting in place a motivating plan for the future. Libby is a powerhouse and I have enjoyed every minute of working with her.

Having dipped my toe into the choreographic waters at the fiftieth anniversary, I was starting to think that I would like to do more. I had long felt that we needed a new version of *The Sleeping Beauty*, one of my favourite ballets and always a winner with audiences. The last production we had staged was Stanton Welch's iteration in 2005, an interesting production, but I felt we needed another, more traditional telling in our repertoire. While we were putting together the post-fiftieth anniversary program, I decided to commission a new *Beauty* for the 2015 season. I had such strong ideas about what I wanted this production to be that I realised I would drive a choreographer completely mad with my parameters and instructions. There was, as always, great pressure for the new production to be a success, and so I started toying with the idea of doing it myself. I discussed it with Nicolette, who was hugely encouraging and floated the idea with the executive team; they also jumped on board. I had a two-day workshop with Nicolette and Patrick McIntyre (who by that stage was executive director of Sydney Theatre Company but remained a great friend), where we picked apart all the reasons to perform a new *Sleeping Beauty*, what the design might look like and the characterisations. I came away from this with a much clearer idea of what I wanted and a sense that I could, in fact, do it, so I set about reading everything I could about the original staging of the ballet and all its versions since. I was elated when the final piece of the puzzle fell into place and designer Gabriela Tylesova agreed to work on the production with me. Creating the ballet – all the fun, fear and excitement it entailed – was the closest I came to experiencing the feelings I had as a dancer.

The production had a budget of $2.5 million, the most expensive ballet the company had ever staged. There were a lot of elaborate scene changes and, with 100 years of sleep to factor in, no recycling of costumes. Kenneth Watkins was extraordinary in garnering support from our generous Ballet family, raising $1.7 million. I tried, with my executive assistant Kate Longley's help, to clear my diary as much as possible for the six weeks leading up to opening night, as I knew how easily day-to-day duties could divert me from the production. Kate was brilliant at running interference on this, but the days were very long and always ended with a string of director jobs to take care of. Another complicating factor was that we had a film crew doing a 'making of' documentary and trailing me around every rehearsal. After a while it was easy to forget they were there; later I was a bit embarrassed to watch the raw footage and see how often I swear under duress. Luckily, much of this was edited out of the final cut – it is a little too revealing to watch hours and hours of yourself working under pressure.

Thankfully, it all came together on opening night and it was a testament to all the people who had worked so hard to make it a success. Thanks to Gabriela the production looked exquisite, Jon Buswell's lighting was radiant, Nicolette and principal pianist Stuart Macklin had led me through the complexities of making cuts to the score without undermining Tchaikovsky's brilliance, Lucas Jervies (choreographer, theatre director and former Australian Ballet dancer) had helped me nut out the dramaturgy, and the orchestra and dancers were superb. I was relieved and thrilled, and very proud of its success. I was even happier to make some revisions to the production in 2017 and take it on successful tours to Beijing and Shanghai in 2018.

With choreographing a full-length ballet now on my CV, what more was there left to do? Wesley had been advising me to leave the company for years, but I hadn't been ready. I always had so many ideas I wanted to bring to fruition. Shortly after Craig Dunn was appointed chair of The Australian Ballet board in 2014, he began to talk to me about succession planning, and I worried this was leading up to me being asked to move on. But he assured me that was not the case, that it was sensible to think about what might happen when the time eventually came. It certainly started me thinking about what I should do. I was now in my fifties and had spent my entire working life with The Australian Ballet, but there were also things I would love to do if I wasn't constrained by a hugely demanding, albeit enjoyable, full-time job. I put together a three-year plan with a lot of big projects on the horizon, but I had to admit to myself that my emotional resilience started to fray a little earlier every year. I loved my job with a passion, but there were aspects of it that had become burdensome. In short, I realised I was worn out.

I mulled over all of this with my friend Margaret Bourke, who very wisely said that there will always be a reason to stay, but you should design your own departure before you have it dictated to you. I had a slew of co-productions in train that were due to be delivered in 2020. I looked at my calendar and realised 2020 would be fifty years since I took my first ballet class in Perth, forty years since I headed east to join The Australian Ballet School, and twenty years since I was appointed artistic director. Who could resist such a line of round numbers? It seemed like the time was right. I went to see Craig and told him that at the end of 2020, I would stand down as artistic director.

CHAPTER 10

Into the open skies

As soon as I told Craig Dunn of my plan to leave at the end of 2020, I regretted it. *What had I done? What would I do without The Australian Ballet?* But I kept those thoughts to myself and slowly worked through them, a kind of pre-emptive grieving process for something that had occupied so much of my heart and mind since I was in primary school. I reached the other side and was content with my decision and the wealth of opportunities it might open up. I wanted to explore more of life (and myself) beyond ballet.

While no artistic directorship is perfect, and there are always things you wish you had done differently or better, I'm very proud of what I have achieved in my twenty years. One of those achievements has been to break down what I call 'Fortress Ballet' – that sense I always had of the company occupying its own world, where few get in and few get out. I could almost imagine a huge drawbridge coming down to occasionally allow people to cross the moat. From my first day as director, I was very keen to change that, both in perception and reality. In my first year, I went to as many dance and arts productions as I could, to see what other companies were doing and how we might fit in a little more with the broader dance ecology. I've tried to open up the company to collaborations and co-productions with other companies, which had started under Ross Stretton's directorship, with the intention of making ballet more accessible to more people. I wanted to demonstrate that we were interested in what other dance companies were doing and were not just an elitist body occupying its own orbit. I think there's still some way to travel on this, but it is somewhat better than it was when I took on the role.

Richard Evans and I also worked hard at creating internal cohesion. When I became director, the company was a particularly siloed operation, with the touring party, the dancers and the administration seemingly operating like separate entities.

We also developed policies across the organisations, and central among these was a proper maternity leave policy. It wasn't very long ago that if a female dancer became pregnant, it more or less ended her performing career. There was no real support for women wanting to return from maternity leave, and the demands of touring and performing at night inevitably proved an impossible juggle with a baby. This left our women, especially the 'ballerina mums', having to effectively choose between a career and a child.

When I came on board as director, there were only six weeks of maternity leave on offer, four days of paternity leave, and no safe duties for women later in their pregnancy. This meant pregnant dancers were really left on their own from fairly early on. We devised the best maternity policy we possibly could. It wasn't just about designing meaningful safe duties – pregnant women could do administrative work or teaching, for example, while still participating in daily class – but supporting them to make sure they weren't disadvantaged in any way by taking time off to have a baby, and could then return to full dancing duties.

We realised that coming back to dancing after having a baby took about nine months – in other words, it took about as long to get back to dancing as it did to have the baby. We came up with sixteen weeks of maternity leave which, when combined with the federal government's paid parental leave, allowed women to take the time they needed without suffering financially. Then we had to think about how to support them when they returned to work and needed to travel, so we hit upon the idea of a children's touring allowance – basically, we would pay the baby to be on tour. This would help in covering childcare or babysitting costs for long tours, such as the two Sydney seasons we do each year. The package didn't cover everything, but it was vastly better than it had been previously and it has seen a lot of babies born to dancers during my time as director! Even better, the mums have come back to performing afterwards. Several of the men have also taken the two weeks' paternity leave.

We also needed to develop an agreed body image policy, to remove some of the anxiety and shame that had gone with it in years gone by. Ballet is an aesthetic art form and requires a certain 'look', but it is also an extremely physically taxing undertaking that requires great strength and stamina. As a dancer, finding a balance in all of this can be difficult. There were times when the emphasis was on being thin, thin, thin, but that was neither healthy nor sustainable with the workloads and diverse repertoire dancers were increasingly expected to perform. Moreover, dancers were often told to 'lose weight' and then left to their own devices, without any support in doing so. I had experienced weight and body image struggles of my own as a dancer, and I felt very uncomfortable, as a male director, coming in and telling the women in particular what their bodies should look like. I spoke with the head of the ballet school, Marilyn Rowe, who said they were having the same issues and were also in need of a proper policy. Thanks to Marilyn, I set up a meeting with Lucinda Sharp, who was in charge of psychology and wellness at the school, and she gave me excellent advice: 'Talk to the dancers and come up with a policy *with* the dancers.'

We did that, discussing the need to be healthy, fit and physically strong, and how we might support the dancers in terms of their physical health. With help from the company's consultant GP, we devised a strategy that we all felt worked. Just as we didn't want dancers carrying too much weight, we also didn't want them to be underweight, and the framework we devised together has proved very successful over the years. There is now a way of approaching this delicate subject and a process to support dancers' health and well-being.

Another important area we also needed to look at was how we could better prevent injuries from occurring, then support dancers to return to work as quickly as responsibly possible when it inevitably did happen. The program of conditioning and strengthening we envisioned complemented our body image and weight policy. Sue Mayes, the company's in-house physiotherapist, worked on putting this program into action. One of the key issues our medical director, Ken Crichton, pointed out was that there was a gap between what the physiotherapists did with injured dancers, and what the dancers were asked to do when they returned to class. In other words, there was a missing link between being 'off' and being 'on'.

We created a permanent position to be the go-between in this dynamic, and I knew from my own experience that Noelle Shader was the perfect person for that role – an experienced teacher with particular expertise in helping injured dancers get back to performance. We then instigated a weekly meeting between medical and dance staff, to better negotiate the tug-of-war between those who wanted a dancer on and those who wanted them off. By managing workload and rehabilitation, we could keep people dancing but not make their injury worse. Sometimes giving a dancer two days of rest was enough to get them back for the remainder of the season, whereas keeping them on for those two days might mean another three months off.

The physical appearance of the dancers all fed into my idea of changing the 'look' of the company. Again, this in part reflected my own experience of being overlooked on occasions because I didn't match the strict classical ideal, something I tried not to let influence my decisions as director. I was also very keen for Australia's flagship ballet company to better reflect the wider community it represents. Ethnic diversity is important, and as the ballet school was taking on kids from a wider range of backgrounds, I wanted that to filter through to the company, too. For example, we gave contracts to more dancers from Japanese backgrounds, as the school was taking in a lot of students from Japan. It took us until 2012 to hire our first Indigenous dancer, Ella Havelka, but we did so and now we have Evie Ferris in the company as well. There is still a way to go with encouraging young dancers from minority backgrounds to feel welcome in ballet schools around the country. Seeing dancers in the company who look like them will only make them feel more motivated to take a local ballet class and aspire to join The Australian Ballet. I look forward to seeing the great richness of ethnicity continue to expand in our ranks.

Early in my directorship, Richard Evans said that if we wanted to build a wider audience for ballet, we needed to get into schools, not just ballet schools. We started to scope out a program that we codenamed Bolte on the Bus, which involved a well-known dancer travelling around schools to do workshops with the students (Lisa Bolte was one of the company's principals). Recognising that we needed some expert help, we brought dance education expert Helen Cameron on board. After much research and consultation, Helen developed a more nuanced program called Out There – The Australian Ballet in Schools, which she ran brilliantly for several years. We have since rebadged this as The Australian Ballet's Education and Outreach Program.

The idea behind the program was to take ballet to kids who might otherwise never be exposed to it; not to teach them to do a perfect plié, but simply to imbue them with a love of dance and movement. The ultimate dream for us was that, in twenty years' time, someone would join the company whose first experience of ballet was the Out There program. It has been a brilliant success: it began in 2006 as a pilot program and has kept building to the point at which it is now a full-time undertaking with four dance educators going into schools.

Another grand idea to introduce ballet to children – especially those who might otherwise never have the opportunity – was called Once Upon a Time. In shortened shows, we performed a section of a well-known story ballet and added a narrator so kids could understand what was going on. It was hugely effective and we realised there was a wider audience for ballets specifically for children. This was reinforced when the *Angelina Ballerina* show based on the best-selling book toured Australia and proved to be box office gold. We talked through a few ideas, including asking some writers to create a ballet specifically for children, but in the end we decided it was best to stick with a shortened, simplified and lively version of our core repertoire. We started with *Storytime Ballet: The Sleeping Beauty* in the summer of 2015–16, which was quite easy to truncate as I'd just staged my version of it. We later did Storytime Ballets of *The Nutcracker* and *Coppélia*, and the ABC released musical versions of *The Sleeping Beauty* and *The Nutcracker* recorded by Orchestra Victoria and conducted by Nicolette, narrated by David Wenham and Geoffrey Rush respectively.

In their small way, I hope these programs help break down the idea in Australia of ballet as an elitist and exclusive art form, and also ensure the next generations of ballet lovers will join us in the theatre. I cannot count the number of times I've met people socially who, after learning of my role at the ballet, have responded with: 'Oh, I don't like ballet.'

'Well,' I usually ask, 'what have you seen?'

'Oh, I'd never go,' they invariably reply. 'I hate it.' I am constantly astonished by people's ability to hate something they have never seen.

Once you get people to buy tickets to the ballet, the trick is to make them want to keep coming back. A large part of this relates to programming, and I am well aware that over the years of my tenure as artistic director, there has been some criticism of my programming as too safe and risk-averse, too focused on the classics and not commissioning enough edgy new works, especially from Australian choreographers. There is probably some degree of truth in this – some years more than others – but my aim has always been to keep the company on safe financial ground and, through that, allow us some artistic freedom to experiment and cushion us if those experiments fail.

From the start, I tried to position myself somewhere between Maina and Ross. Maina's programming was primarily traditional, featuring a preference and love for the great 19th-century classical ballets, with wings and eyelashes and tulle as far as the eye could see. When Ross took over, it was like going from the sauna to the ice bath; he brought in lots of avant-garde new works that were cutting-edge but inevitably alienated some in the audience, especially those who loved the big story ballets. But Ross built an audience for those works, often younger people, and I certainly didn't want to lose them. I tried to forge a middle path because, as I always joke, if I'd commissioned wall-to-wall nude ballets, our subscribers would have deserted us and my directorship would have been very short-lived. Similarly, if I'd only done the big tutu ballets, we would never garner new subscribers and we'd erode our support base.

Moreover, the dancers want to dance a mixed program. They are interested in the contemporary works that really challenge them technically, and not always in the high classical way; equally, they want to dance the big story ballets and have the chance to be Aurora or Siegfried or the Sugar Plum Fairy, using the technique that they have studied since childhood. Likewise, if we do too many big ballets, the dancers complain of being bored and ask when we're going to do more cutting-edge ballets.

Works that are put on the same bill have to make sense in some way – the program needs to be carefully created so the mix is not too jarring. I've always tried to give any mixed bill a name that ties them all together, and not one we have used before, otherwise people think they've already seen it. *Mixed Bill* or *Triple Bill* are deeply unsexy names for performances, so we worked hard to come up with names that made sense and were also enticing: *20:21*, *Bella*, *Icons* and *Chroma* were examples of this.

Along with breadth, I tried to add depth, and Nicolette Fraillon and Patrick McIntyre were enormously influential in this. With our

Balanchine program, *Mr B*, we pulled together very diverse works, so audiences could see the different styles of one choreographer. The Jiří Kylián program was similar – all masterpieces, but audiences saw an early-, middle- and late-career work. It was all about exposing people to new works and ideas, and we commissioned many writers to flesh out the programs and delve into the works we were doing and why we were doing them. That was the reason the Ballets Russes project, which was Nicolette's baby, ran for four years – we had the opportunity to really educate people about our dance history, and celebrate the evolution of classical ballet in Australia.

I have certainly made some programming mistakes along the way. When I first started as artistic director, I erred too much on the safe side, and we played to audiences at 60 to 70 per cent capacity. These days, our capacity most years is around 86 to 87 per cent. Audiences vote with their feet and they have liked what we do. I don't think we've performed boring work – Wayne McGregor's *Dyad 1929* was a huge success, and some of the reimaginations of classical works have been warmly received as well. I think dance writers sometimes think we have done more 19th-century classical ballets than we actually have.

The big regret I have from my time as director is that I haven't commissioned a great, full-length, original Australian ballet to forever hold a place in the repertoire. I had a 'code' name for this elusive work in my future planning wish list: *Secret River, the Ballet*, a tribute to the extraordinary Kate Grenville novel that was transformed into such a compelling piece of theatre. I loved that adaptation and would have loved to find another equally captivating piece of literature that could be adapted as successfully into a unique new ballet. But I never did find that great Australian story, and not for lack of trying. When we were nearing the fiftieth anniversary, we held a competition: pitch us an iconic Australian work that is crying out to be done. When the ideas came in, though, people were pitching things like Hans Christian Andersen's *Snow Queen*, which was baffling. We didn't discover the big narrative work that made us sit up and say, 'Oh my god, that's *it*.' Nicolette and I had constant discussions along these lines. We'd say: what about this idea or that one, but we were never completely inspired by any of them. Then there was always the problem of finding a choreographer who was equally stimulated by the idea, and often they weren't.

Another disappointment is that I wish I had been less inclined to give in to financial pressures at the expense of artistic ambition. My deep love of pleasing people has been a double-edged sword, and not pushing back on the organisation and the board in the name of taking a few risks is one area where it has not always served me well. The Australian Ballet is wonderfully well run by its management and its board, but there were times when potentially great works were abandoned because of financial priorities. There is always a risk when staging newer or less well-known ballets, and I have also commissioned my fair share of underperforming ballets. But happenstance is at the heart of the creative process, and that is often something that boards struggle to get their heads around. My hope is that the next artistic director is willing to push hard for the projects they really believe in, even if it challenges the bottom line.

The Australian Ballet is a world-class company, expertly run, and something of which Australians should be very proud. My great dream is that one day Australians will feel as excited and proud of their flagship ballet company as they do of their Olympic or cricket teams, but there is some way to travel on that. We have produced some extraordinary artists in this country who are recognised around the globe, and we should revel in the richness of our artistic and creative landscape.

Ballet classes for children remain overwhelmingly female. Although we now encourage our girls to believe they can do anything at all, we haven't yet reached this point with boys – and that is a shame. I look at a country like Cuba or Russia, where dance is such an integral part of the culture and kids dance from the time they can walk, and I wish even a little of that could make its way to Australia. Too often I still hear stories of boys – even the really gifted ones who end up in the company – coming to dance by accident, and being teased the way I was, or hiding the fact that they do ballet. In recent years, I have seen signs this is starting to shift, so I hope it continues to do so.

I feel so positive about the future of the company, especially now that I am handing the reins on to David Hallberg. Apart from being one of the most recognised male dancers in the world, who has danced with every major ballet company, David has built a strong affinity with The Australian Ballet over the past decade. Since arriving as a guest artist in 2010, he immediately felt like one of us, and this was cemented when he spent fourteen months with the company in 2015–16 while recovering from major surgery on his ankle.

I told David when he was appointed that I was as excited as I had been when I was appointed, and it is the truth. It is wonderful to know that the company will be led into the future by David, with his abundant humanity and integrity backed by the most diverse and rich experiences as a dancer. The only slightly cumbersome problem was the confusion of Davids when talking about the artistic director both coming and going. The very elegant solution we came up with was to be 'David 7' and 'David 8', the order of our succession – I was the seventh director and David will be the eighth. (I hatched a sneaky plan to be referred to as 'David 007' for the transition.)

What a period of transition it has been. With all guns blazing, we started our first season of 2020 in Brisbane with the world premiere of Graeme Murphy's *The Happy Prince*, which heralded the start of a huge line-up of repertoire that boasted two other new full-evening narrative ballets. We then returned to Melbourne to prepare our next world premiere, this time *Logos* by resident choreographer Alice Topp, which was part of the *Volt* triple bill bookended by two masterworks by Wayne McGregor: *Chroma* and *Dyad 1929*. As we approached the opening night, the shadow of the COVID-19 pandemic was starting to close in on Australia. After only three performances, the theatres were closed and 'social distancing' entered our daily lexicon. The year 2020 very quickly became one that the whole world would never forget.

The company responded quickly and nimbly. Technology was swiftly put in place to enable the organisation to work from home, and each day the dancers were able to log on to our video conferencing platform and take classes. The entertainment industry was completely struck down. The whole country went into a weird sort of hibernation. Nightly television news reports from around the globe relay the tragedy and heartache this pandemic has caused, the hardships so many endure. For many of us, COVID-19 has made time to take stock and think. The very best and, at times, the baser traits of humanity are laid bare. I can see that this will fundamentally change the world, and I really do hope that we emerge with a more generous and enlightened outlook.

We titled 2020 the 'Year of Limitless Possibilities'. Little did we know the many ways in which our creativity and resilience would be tested. I am proud of the spirited response to the changing daily landscape from every part of the organisation, and grateful for the amazing support our company has received from our stakeholders: government and corporate partners, donors and audience members. We have been able to give audiences around Australia access to a curated program of past performances online through our At Home with Ballet TV digital season, including lots of behind-the-scenes footage and photos. Even the little Dancing with David videos on the social channels have received great feedback from a wide audience who are discovering pliés and spring points in the comfort of their own homes. One certainty is that when this crisis comes to an end and we emerge from our physical isolation, artists will be the ones to bring joy back into people's lives and help reunite communities. As we have over the past almost sixty years, I know The Australian Ballet will be there to stimulate audiences with our performances and use the transformative power of dance to inspire those around us to thrive once again.

Following this unprecedented time, how do I untangle myself from The Australian Ballet? Not in any permanent way – I could never leave it forever – but in a very tangible way that allows David Hallberg to put his stamp on the company and also allows me to keep building my identity away from it. When I finally made the decision to leave, Wesley gave me some great advice: to build a 'boat' in my mind in which I could sail away both physically and emotionally.

The first physical opportunity to do that came via my great friend Madeleine Onne, who is the artistic director of the Finnish National Ballet. We met at the 'rural retreat' in 2003, when Madeleine was artistic director at the Royal Swedish Ballet, and stayed in touch over the years. When I rang to congratulate her on her appointment in Finland, she mentioned she was commissioning a new *Swan Lake* to commemorate the company's 100th anniversary in 2022. We talked a little about who might do it, and then she mentioned, 'I would like the production to be something like what you did with *The Sleeping Beauty*.'

I didn't want to put her in an awkward position if she was just 'spitballing', as the Americans say, but *was* she dropping a hint? That night I talked about it with Wesley, and he suggested sending Madeleine an email asking if I could send her some ideas. I did that, and after several conversations and a couple of trips to Finland, I was commissioned to choreograph a new *Swan Lake* for the Finnish National Ballet. Once again I am working with the splendid Gabriela Tylesova, who will design the sets and costumes, and Kalle Ropponen, a hugely talented Finnish lighting designer who will complete the creative team. My timeframe is tight – it all begins in the studio about a month after I finish with The Australian Ballet, so it will be something to look forward to and a great distraction from the grief I might feel at leaving. I hope there will be more opportunities like this to work with ballet companies in some capacity, but I guess that will depend on how it goes.

I want to explore non-ballet ambitions as well. I intend to take drawing classes and record some of my experiences with pencil and paper rather than on my mobile phone's camera. I have always wanted to sew, having spent so much time watching my mum make clothes for us when I was a kid. Similarly, while I've been at the Ballet, I've invariably enjoyed heading down to the wardrobe department to watch costumes come to life. I'd love to grab some materials and see what I can do with them.

I'm also really looking forward to seeing more of the world as a tourist rather than travelling to places solely for work. While one doesn't imagine the world will automatically go back to the way it was before COVID-19, with travellers perfectly free to satisfy their wanderlust in just about any way they wished, I hope that Wesley and I will be able to spend time in Europe in the future and visit places I've never holidayed in before. All things being well, I would love to spend time, unhurried, sitting in small squares at the centre of various cities and soaking up the surrounding history, maybe doing some sketches. This travel will hopefully also give me the opportunity to catch up with all the wonderful friends I have made, all over the world, whom I haven't seen enough of due to the demands of my job. I often joke that I see more of the company's donors than I do of my friends – fortunately, many of those donors have become great friends as well.

And I have Wesley by my side. Our relationship is into its second decade now, and I'm looking forward to us becoming old men together. (He likes to remind me that many people think we already are.) We are fairly well known as a couple in the Australian arts community, and in recent years have done some media together (although we are still hardly ever in the same place at the same time, and when we are, we usually just hang out together at home). As the marriage equality vote in Australia drew near in 2017, we were asked to appear in an article together expressing our views. We were obviously very supportive of marriage equality, and while we've talked a bit about whether we'd ever tie the knot ourselves, we're yet to decide. Still, it is important that we and all couples have the equal opportunity to do that. We were so relieved the plebiscite was such a resounding success for the 'yes' vote.

I have learnt a lot from Wesley, and he has given me a much broader view of our industry and our country. He has also been extremely supportive of my career, even when that support has been uncomfortable: he, more than anyone, has challenged my thinking and helped me make more clear-headed decisions. He's been a great sounding-board for creative ideas, too. I'll never forget him sitting patiently while I danced around the lounge room working on scenes for my *Sleeping Beauty* in 2015; fortunately, he was smart enough to have his bluetooth headphones with him so as not to hear too much Tchaikovsky on high repeat. He is my biggest supporter, but also pushes me to think big and engage with new ideas and opportunities.

At home, we have settled into a Yin and Yang routine that works well. Wesley is a brilliant cook, so I'm looking forward to us entertaining frequently, with him doing the cooking and me doing the tidying and cleaning. Wesley loves argument and debate, whereas I'm more a fan of the quiet life – I'll be the one looking for the place of consensus and calm. Much to his annoyance, we rarely argue, as I just walk away. He's much better at prosecuting an argument than I am, and anyway, I'm pretty easygoing on most things. Holidays can be challenging: Wesley gets bored easily, while I can spend hours reading, watching television and doing very little. I think the best holidays for us will be when our diaries intersect for part of a trip, but the rest of it we spend alone. We are both quite content in our own company.

We have bought a place together in Melbourne, and hopefully we'll spend some time in it. When we do, I will be the Lord of the Laundry – I am fastidious about washing and ironing and have a strict policy on separating whites from colours. Sometimes I go to Sydney and spend the afternoon simply ironing Wesley's shirts; I also iron sheets, to his great amusement. But is there a better feeling than jumping in between freshly laundered and ironed sheets? I don't think so.

The end of my formal ballet journey has allowed me to reflect very happily on that uncomfortable conversation I had with Kelvin as a nineteen-year-old, when he told me to sort myself out. I'm still a work in progress and I've made a lot of missteps along the way, but I can honestly say I think I might finally have found peace with myself. Looking back at that confused young man, I wish I could give him some advice: search for what makes you happy, not for what other people think ought to make you happy. And when you find it, be gentle with yourself.

I'll always be involved in ballet in some way. I'll be in the audience, watching the company grow and delighting in each new wave of talented young dancers. I'll see them push themselves, cast aside pain, search for something more, better, deeper. I'll rejoice when they transport the audience, reveal a human truth, or simply demonstrate the extraordinary capacity of the human body. It is what great art does – it makes us better people, and the world a better place. It helps us soar.

Acknowledgements

There have been a number of times in my life when I have achieved things I never thought possible, and this book sits firmly in that category! I want to thank Amanda Dunn, who originally floated the idea of this memoir and who has been such a joy to work with in writing it. I will miss our time chatting together, a sort of literary therapy where so many strands of my life came together to weave this story and, in the process, reveal the logic of why I am who I am.

It has also been a great pleasure to work with everyone at Thames & Hudson Australia, whose expertise and guidance have been invaluable – especially associate publisher Sally Heath, whose editorial eye and personal warmth and belief in telling this tale has been such a great support. I also loved my virtual time with copy editor Meaghan Amor, whom I look forward to meeting in person post–COVID-19 social distancing (which was in force as we worked on the book together), and editor Jessica Levine, who did all the final wrangling to bring this book into being. To all the photographers whose work is represented here and shows so vividly the various phases of my career, thank you for your generosity in allowing me to publish it. Equally, to those I have mentioned within these pages: you have all shared my path at different stages, and I want to thank you for your friendship, guidance and companionship.

As a proud graduate of The Australian Ballet School who was lucky enough to be part of The Australian Ballet for the past thirty-eight years, I want to express my gratitude to the company for enabling me to have the most fulfilling career! It was Dame Margaret Scott who gave me that first opportunity to go to the ABS, and from there Maina Gielgud and the remarkable team at The Australian Ballet nurtured my career. I have been fortunate enough to have two 'dream' jobs, and the most rewarding time in both.

I want to thank everyone at The Australian Ballet for being such an inspiration over the past thirty-eight years and for genuinely making getting up each morning a pleasure. To Libby Christie, whose passion and energy has no end and with whom I have loved sharing the CEO role for the past eight years. To the board of The Australian Ballet and all the chairs (Mel Ward, David Crawford, Christopher Knoblanche, Jim Cousins and Craig Dunn) who have been there to offer guidance and support. To my fellow members of the executive team past and present, whose collective brains trust has made us so successful over all these years, but especially to Nicolette Fraillon, Kenneth Watkins, Richard Evans, Patrick McIntyre, Philippe Magid, Sally Underwood, Penny Rowland, Penny Waitsman, Kate Scott, Francis Croese, Angela Embleton, Yvonne Gates, Helen McCormack and Chris Yates – it was a hell of a lot of fun working with you! In preparation for this book, the ballet company once again were there to offer support and encouragement. A special thank you to Rose Mulready, who ran her expert eye over the final manuscript, and to Donna Cusack-Muller, Renee Colquhoun, Marie MacGregor, Anthea Waller, Sophie Rennard, Emma Pinwill and her team.

In my time as artistic director, I have learnt the liberating power of asking for help. I have been so lucky to have the most extraordinary executive assistants along the way who have made it possible for me to do my job and keep sane. Megan Connelly (who taught me I didn't need to do the photocopying, and so much more), Emily O'Connor and Larissa McKinnon, you all enabled me to take on the challenges I faced as artistic director, and you have my deepest gratitude for putting up with me. I have most recently enjoyed a wonderful partnership with executive assistant Kate Longley, whom amazingly I have never seen become angry – and goodness knows I have given her every opportunity to do so! Several of the photographs within these pages are hers, and she has made time for me to write this book and still do my day job while keeping me rational with her friendship. Since Kate has been on maternity leave, Eloise Fryer has stepped in seamlessly to help me navigate the way through delivering on all that I said I would, once again with great humour and support.

To all the dancers and ballet staff, you are the engine room of The Australian Ballet, and your creativity, dedication and talent has fuelled my work at the company through both my careers. My fellow dancers, and then the generations who joined under my leadership, thank you for always inspiring me and thrilling the audiences who have marvelled at your artistry and brilliance on stage. To the ballet staff, thank you for making me a better dancer and then supporting me as artistic director. I would especially like to thank Petal Miller-Ashmole, Noelle Shader, Colin Peasley, Ai-Gul Gaisina, Wang Jiahong, Jonathan Kelly and Gary Norman, who nurtured and coached me during my dance career. Thank you to Danilo Radojevic, Fiona Tonkin, Wendy Walker, Mark Kay, Franco Leo, Karen Blissett, Elizabeth Hill, Eve Lawson, Tristan Message, Steven Heathcote, Elizabeth Toohey, Paul Knobloch, Megan Connelly, Kismet Bourne, Alex Wyatt, Eloise Fryer, Caitlin Topham, Robyn Begg and

Amelia Drummond, whose work enabled the artistic program to dazzle so brilliantly during my directorship.

Dance needs music, and I have had the pleasure of working every day, as both dancer and director, with some of the best musical artists from across the country and around the globe. Conductors Noel Smith, John Lanchbery, Barry Wordsworth, Ormsby Wilkins, Peter Bandy, Bryan Stacey and of course Nicolette Fraillon have been a few of the maestros with whom I was fortunate enough to perform and collaborate. The daily inspiration from fantastic ballet pianists such as Wendy Pomroy, Stuart Macklin, Emma Lippa, Duncan Salton, Brian Cousins and Kylie Foster, along with so many others, is how I managed to make sense of the movement and, in so many classes and rehearsals, gain the strength to keep going.

To the medical teams who treated me – especially Ken Crichton, Karim Khan, Sarah Way, Mike Ralston, Sten Liljedahl, Andrew Baxter, Janet Brown, Paulette Mifsud and Zara Gomes – thank you for keeping me dancing for SO long. Over these past twenty years, The Australian Ballet's artistic health team has led the world and nurtured our dancers' health and well-being through innovative treatments underpinned by evidence-based research. Thank you to the team, formed and led by Dr Sue Mayes in collaboration with doctors Andrew Garnham, Seamus Dalton, Vicki Higgins, Sonya Morrison and a group of exceptional physiotherapists and health professionals including Sophie Emery, Sam Wright, Shaun Bryce, Sakis Michelis and Sarah Thompson.

I wanted to share details of my personal story in this book, as I have tended to focus on my career in the public arena. I'd like to thank everyone from my 'private' world who has allowed me to reveal our shared lives. The search for my most authentic self has been a journey that I have undertaken with many wonderful people, and I really thank you all, those mentioned in these pages and those who aren't, for being there with me. A special thanks goes to Margaret Bourke, Fred Conway, Nerida O'Loughlin, Sarah and Mike Ralston, Robyn Fynmore, Darren Spowart, Stuart Macklin, Margaret Fitzsimmons, Tim Foley and Louise Ward.

I also want to thank my wonderful family. Mum and Dad, I dedicate this book to you, and while Mum won't get to read it, Dad, you have always been a rock and allowed me to be myself, which I am sure was not easy at times. To my brothers, Phillip, Paul and James, it has been a joy to share our lives with one another, especially through the tough times when being the brother of the 'ballet boy' was a poisoned chalice. I look forward to all that our shared future holds. To my sister, Dianne, from playing together with dolls and Fuzzy-Felt, through dress-ups and teenage angst, and now as adults – you are so dear to me, and I love that we still get to share secrets and navigate the world together. To my extended family – Ashley Morris and beautiful nieces Amy and Charlotte Morris, Steve Mummery, Emma McAllister and Ednamay Foston – you have all brought such personal riches to the clan. To my wonderful partner, Wesley, thank you for always trying to make sense of the world, indulging my laundry addiction and being my lover and friend. I look forward to growing old with you (fingers crossed).

To all who have been with me through my career and life, thank you. These pages are forever fraught with the fear of not including everyone who walked someway along the path with me and helped decipher the mysteries of life. To be a performer is to be surrounded by people who validate what we do. Audience members, philanthropists, silent ballet admirers, critics, dance teachers and fellow industry folk, you have all witnessed my time in this wonderful creative world. To all of you who have been there and continue that encouragement by showing interest in my story told here, I really appreciate your support.

Here's to everyone who dreams big and dances like there is nothing more important to do in life. May we all enjoy a healthy and creative future.

Index